THE ISRAELI REPUBLIC: JALAL AL-E AHMAD, ISLAM, AND THE JEWISH STATE

Translated from the Persian by Samuel Thrope,
with essays by Samuel Thrope and Bernard Avishai

RESTLESS BOOKS
Brooklyn, New York

THE ISRAELI REPUBLIC:
JALAL AL-E AHMAD, ISLAM, AND THE JEWISH STATE

*Among the Believers: What Jalal Al-E Ahmad Thought
Iranian Islamism Could Learn from Zionism* by Bernard Avishai was
originally published in *Foreign Affairs*, Vol. 39, No. 2, March/April 2014

First Restless Books paperback edition January 2017

ISBN: 978-1-63206-139-3
Library of Congress Control Number: 2016940770

Cover design by Daniel Benneworth-Gray

Printed in the United States of America
1 3 5 7 9 8 6 4 2

Ellison, Stavans, and Hochstein LP
232 3rd Street, Suite A111
Brooklyn, NY 11215

www.restlessbooks.com
publisher@restlessbooks.com

CONTENTS

INTRODUCTION

BY SAMUEL THROPE

IN THE FALL of 1964 a twenty-five-year-old clerical seminary student named Ali Khamenei—who would become, ten years after the 1979 Islamic Revolution, supreme leader of Iran—placed an angry phone call to Jalal Al-e Ahmad.

Al-e Ahmad, Iran's leading writer and one of the foremost critics of Shah Mohammad Reza Pahlavi's rule, had just two years before published his most enduring work, *Gharbzadegi*, a scathing attack on the regime, which had endeared himself to the shah's religious opposition. Best translated in English as "Occidentosis" (the state of being afflicted by the disease of the West), this profoundly influential essay, which became a watchword in Iranian politics, called on Iranians to abandon Westernization and return to their cultural roots in Islam.

A new article, however had rattled the seminarians—chief among them Ayatollah Ruhollah Khomeini, the revolutionary cleric, founder of the Islamic Republic, and Khamenei's mentor. That article was "Journey to the Land of Israel," an account of—and justification for—Al-e Ahmad's week-long trip to Israel in February of 1963.

The early 1960s was a tumultuous time in Iran. In the face of increasing unrest and student protests, in 1963 the shah unveiled a sweeping and unprecedented set of social and industrial reforms, known together as the White Revolution, that aimed to rapidly industrialize and modernize Iran; a key provision of these reforms, which garnered particular clerical opposition, was universal women's suffrage. A controversial referendum on the reforms came just weeks before Al-e Ahmad's journey to Israel, and was challenged by Khomeini, who orchestrated a short-lived clerical uprising that resulted in his exile in 1964. Khomeini would not return until after the shah fled Iran amid the revolutionary fervor of 1979.

In Ali Khamenei's later recollection of their phone conversation, he emphasized his continuing admiration for Al-e Ahmad despite "the discontent and objection ["Journey to the Land of Israel"] raised in me and many of the hopeful youth of those days." As they spoke, he writes, "the intelligence, affection, purity, and suffering of a man who in those days was at the pinnacle of opposition literature crashed over me like a wave."[1]

What about the article, then, had made the seminarian so angry? Khamenei was, surely, upset that Al-e Ahmad had visited Israel and written positively about the country. While other Iranian intellectuals had traveled to the Jewish State, Al-e Ahmad was the best-known and highest-profile writer to have done so.

Furthermore, relations between Tehran and Jerusalem were growing in the late 1950s and '60s. Though the shah never formally recognized Israel, military, intelligence, and economic ties between the countries became increasingly close: Iranians were treated as medical tourists in Israeli hospitals, and a growing number of Israeli advisers and contractors resided in Tehran. To the consternation of Iran's Arab neighbors, and the internal religious opposition, the strategic partnership between Israel and Iran, two non-Arab American-allied states, was becoming stronger. For Khamenei, like his teacher Ayatollah Khomeini, this alliance was another example of the shah's perfidiousness, pandering to the West, and enmity towards Islam.

However, what must have struck the young Khamenei about "Journey to the Land of Israel"—and what remains striking to this day—is not only that Al-e Ahmad praised the Jewish State, but how he chose to do so. Al-e Ahmad's text is infused with a particularly Shia Muslim religious language, drawing on the same traditions that served Ayatollah Khomeini and others in conceptualizing the theological politics that would be realized in the Islamic Republic. In all his work, Al-e Ahmad, a cleric's son who had studied in religious seminaries before breaking with Islamic practice in his youth, writes with a command of the classical sources and the religious idiom. But Al-e Ahmad applies that knowledge in a radical way: the Jews and their non-Muslim—or, as some would say, anti-Muslim—state are presented and praised in terms usually reserved for righteous clerics, religious pageants, and the twelve holy Shia imams. He calls Israel a *velayat*: a term describing a model state shepherded by clerical guardians, less than prophets but much more than politicians. In contrast, Arab states, including Saudi Arabia (the location of the holy cities of Mecca and Medina), are dismissed as puppets of the West and slaves to the oil companies. Al-e Ahmad's Israel is posited, provocatively, if not unambiguously, as the ideal Muslim government.

The book that grew out of that 1964 article (which makes up the book's first two chapters) was edited and published by Al-e Ahmad's brother Shams as *Journey to the Land of the Angel of Death* in 1984, five years after the Islamic Revolution and fifteen years after the author's death in 1969. However, the phrase "land of the angel of death" appears nowhere in Al-e Ahmad's text. Rather than choosing between the title of Al-e Ahmad's original article and the title given to the published book, we have chosen the title *The Israeli Republic*.

Al-e Ahmad's work reminds us of Israel and Iran's close prerevolutionary relationship, easy to forget when seen through the lens of recent threats and mutual recrimination; it is almost impossible to imagine an Iranian intellectual of his stature visiting Israel today, much less on a trip organized and paid for by the Israeli government. The fact that Al-e Ahmad is a canonical writer who was admired by the leaders of the Islamic Revolution makes his appreciation of Israel all the more uncanny and titillating. It is tempting to relegate this book to the status of a curiosity, a nostalgic memorial to the two countries cooperation under the shah.

Al-e Ahmad's insights, though, are not only of historical value. *The Israeli Republic* turns on a still-illuminating metaphor—mentioned above—likening Israel to the ideal Muslim state. This bold and surprising comparison opens the door for thinking differently about, and seeing the similarities between, Zionism and the Islamic Republic, political Judaism and political Islam. For behind this metaphor is a deeper question that, for all Al-e Ahmad's stress on the Jewish State's characteristics as an Islamic utopia, remains unresolved in *The Israeli Republic*. Just as importantly, it is a question still unresolved in Israel's conception of itself: Is it East, or is it West?

These categories deserve some explanation. East and West are central notions in Al-e Ahmad's thinking. In his seminal critique *Gharbzadegi*, first published just before his journey to Israel, East and West are taken not as geographical or political designations, as in the Eastern and Western blocs of the Cold War, but as cultural and economic concepts. Western nations, which from Al-e Ahmad's perspective includes the countries of North America and Europe, as well as South Africa and the Soviet Union, have high wages, social services, "nominal democracy," low mortality, low fertility, and mechanization; they are the global producers. Eastern nations, the global consumers, have just the opposite characteristics. "The West compromises the sated nations," he writes, "and the East, the hungry nations."[2] It is a radically dualist division.

In Al-e Ahmad's analysis, Iran is part of the East and is infected by the West. In his diagnosis Iranian society, in particular the intellectual class, was overrun by the West and Western culture, feverish for its products, and aping its wealth and lifestyle. While the shah's vision of Iran as an integral part of European—or, in his terms, Aryan—culture was one of the causes of the disease, Al-e Ahmad's analysis of gharbzadegi was not limited to the court or certain political classes; he saw it as a disease of society as a whole. In particular, Al-e Ahmad argues that Iran's rapid industrialization, guided by Western experts—the "embrace of the machine," as he calls it—and the subsequent rise in consumption and consumer capitalism, were enslaving Iran to imported Western technology and ripping apart its traditional social fabric. Al-e Ahmad acknowledges that the process of mechanization can not be reversed, and contends that the cure entails wresting control of "the machine" from foreign hands: "One must have the machine; one must build it," he writes. "But one must not remain in bondage to it; one must not fall into its snare." The way to avoid bondage is to return to the firm roots of Iranian culture—the most important among them Shia Islam.

The Israeli Republic should be read in light of these concerns and prescriptions, and *Gharbzadegi*'s radical division of East and West. Al-e Ahmad's interest in Israel arose because the Jewish State presented an alternative model, a mix of Western industry and native culture of the sort he advocates in *Gharbzadegi*. However, even from the beginning, his view of Israel was ambiguous. In *The Israeli Republic*, Al-e Ahmad speaks with two voices. On the one hand, Israel is painted as an Eastern and Islamic utopia, a part of the East "of which one end is Tel Aviv and the other Tokyo," and where the division between East and West has been overcome. In Al-e Ahmad's rosy and naive depiction of Israeli society, Ashkenazi Jews from Europe and America and Sephardi Jews from the Middle East and North Africa are integrated into one common, Hebrew culture. On the other, Israel is derided as "the sure bridgehead of Western capitalism" in the East and "a coursely realized indemnity" for the Holocaust: "that is the West's sin and I, an Easterner, am paying the price."

The difference is greatest between the first four chapters, which include the article that so angered Khamenei as well as Al-e Ahmad's further reflections on his 1963 journey, and the last, written after Israel's victory over Egypt, Syria, and Jordan, and conquest of the West Bank, Gaza Strip, Golan Heights, and Sinai Peninsula in the 1967 Six-Day War. Like many other Iranian intellectuals, the 1967 war prompted Al-e Ahmad to change his opinion on Israel. While the first chapters praise Israel as model for overcoming gharbzadegi, the final chapter, presented as a letter to Al-e Ahmad from a friend in Paris, condemns Israeli aggression and the cover European intellectuals provide for its crimes. Using familiar anti-Semitic tropes, this support is blamed on Jews' secret control of banks, the media, and government. Even here, though, Al-e Ahmad is not univocal. Alongside comparisons between Zionism and Nazism, the chapter calls on Israelis and Palestinians to follow Martin Buber's proposal for a federated Jewish-Arab state, and condemns as demagoguery Arab threats to push Israel into the sea.

There is reason to be suspicious of this final chapter's true intentions. Though some have argued that it is a forgery propagated by Shams Al-e Ahmad, Jalal Al-e Ahmad's brother who edited and published *The Israeli Republic*, the chapter's epistolary structure implies that the opinions expressed are those of a character, Al-e Ahmad's literary invention. The chapter also includes a prefatory note that can be taken as a warning to distinguish between the letter writer and Al-e Ahmad's additions: "the nonsense and beard-pulling" of the letter, Al-e Ahmad writes, "are mine; the serious assertions his."

However we interpret the final chapter's harshest statements, though, reading *The Israeli Republic* as a whole Al-e Ahmad's deep ambiguity comes to the fore. Considering what was at stake, Al-e Ahmad's ultimate inability to decide is not surprising. Determining Israel's alignment with East or West was, on one level, a pressing political and cultural question not only for him but other Iranian intellectuals: Could Zionism really serve as a model for the remedy that Iran required? Just as importantly, as a Muslim, an Easterner, and an intellectual opposed to the shah's policies, which included close relations with Israel, how should he relate to the Jewish State's existence in the heart of the Muslim Middle East?

On another level, though, this question was deeply personal. Mapping Israel's Easterness and Westerness was a means, one of many he explored in his life, for struggling with his own place between these two poles. In *Gharbzadegi* Al-e Ahmad rails against Westernization, but he himself was an example of precisely the kind of Westernized intellectual he derides: a non-practicing Muslim, a leftist, a devotee and translator of Western writers like Sartre and Camus, who spoke French and had traveled widely in Europe. In Israel, and in particular in the socialist collective farms known as kibbutzim, Al-e Ahmad recognized a form, redemptive and dramatic, that might resolve his personal and cultural crisis. It was because Israel mattered to him that Al-e Ahmad praised it with such enthusiasm and, later, condemned it with such vitriol, and the reason that both his enthusiasm and his vitriol remained ambiguous and unresolved.

Al-e Ahmad had a long history of enthusiasm and disappointment. In a 1964 essay titled "My Husband, Jalal," his wife Simin Daneshvar—a literature professor at the university of Tehran and important novelist in her own right who accompanied him on his Israel trip—identifies restlessness, or adventurousness, as Al-e Ahmad's essential characteristic. Al-e Ahmad ran from ideology to ideology: from a traditional religious upbringing, he fled to the Marxism of the Tudeh Party, and from there to disaffected Communist writers like Arthur Koestler and André Gide, to Iran's villages, to gharbzadegi, to Israel, and to Islam. In so doing he did not follow trends, but set them. Al-e Ahmad has been described rightly as the bellwether of Iranian intellectuals, and of Iranian society as a whole. His eventual disappointment with each of his intellectual enthusiasms, a chain of disenchantment cut short by his death in 1969, was similarly felt by other Iranians struggling to find their places in a society torn between tradition and modernity, Islam and the West, freedom and authority. It was his willingness to struggle and to fail, and fail honestly, that made Al-e Ahmad the leading literary intellectual of his day.

* * *

Jalal Al-e Ahmad was born in Tehran in 1923. His father, a brother, and two brothers-in-law were all trained as clerics (known by the title "mullah" in Iran), and he was more distantly related to Ayatollah Mahmoud Taleghani, who would become an important religious opponent to the shah's regime. After finishing primary school, Al-e Ahmad was sent to work in Tehran's bazaar and to study at the Marvi Madreseh, where he received the foundations of a traditional religious education; secretly, without his par ents' knowledge, Al-e Ahmad also studied at night at Iran's leading European-style high school, the Dar al-Fanun, where he obtained his diploma in 1943.

In 1941, Britain and Russia invaded and deposed the ruler Reza Shah, who had declared neutrality in World War II and refused to allow Allied transport across Iranian territory. Though Iran was once again under the heel of foreign powers, a recurring theme since the early nineteenth century, one of the unintended consequences of the Allies' invasion was a new political openness. After deposing the last Qajar king in 1925, Reza Shah had become increasingly despotic, banning political parties, imprisoning opponents, censoring literature, and violating Iran's 1906 constitution. With his departure, censorship was lifted, and nationalist, radical, socialist, and Marxist parties and publications roared into life. By 1943 there were forty-seven newspapers in Tehran, each associated with a political party—in a city of only 750,000 inhabitants, many of whom were illiterate.

During his student years, Al-e Ahmad avidly absorbed this radical literature, especially the work of the former cleric, turned militant secularist, Ahmad Kasravi. Al-e Ahmad abandoned his plans for a clerical career, and, after a period of investigating the various political parties, joined the Communist Tudeh party in 1944. This decision resulted in a sharp break with his family. Left to his own resources, Al-e Ahmad attended Tehran's Teacher Training College. He would work off and on as a teacher throughout his life, and his interest in education is reflected in his discussion of Israel's schools in *The Israeli Republic*.

Al-e Ahmad quickly rose through the ranks of the Tudeh, becoming a member of the party's Tehran central committee, and editor and contributor for several of its newspapers and magazines. His first collection of stories, *An Exchange of Visits*, was culled from these periodicals and published in 1946, followed by another collection, *Our*

Suffering, the next year. These two volumes, along with a third collection from 1948 called *Sehtar*, established Al-e Ahmad's reputation as Iran's leading postwar writer.

His fiction depicts the everyday lives of Iranians left behind—or simply left bewildered—by modernization and Westernization. Often set in working-class South Tehran, the same poor section of the city where Al-e Ahmad himself grew up, these stories are, with a few exceptions, drawn from his own life experience. "My Sister and the Spider," a story about a girl dying of cancer narrated by her younger brother, is retold as an event in Al-e Ahmad's own youth in his memoir *A Stone on a Grave*. The 1958 novel *The School Principal*, widely considered his most successful work of fiction, closely mirrors Al-e Ahmad's own experiences running a provincial elementary school.

A large measure of his reputation is due to his innovative style. In his early stories, and even more so in his mature works, Al-e Ahmad speaks through detached narrators; in this he may owe something to existentialist French writers like Sartre, Camus, and Ionesco, authors whose work he translated into Persian. Al-e Ahmad's Persian is spare, condensed, and unadorned, mostly lacking the elaborate allusions to classical literature common in more conventional prose. Instead, Al-e Ahmad's fiction (and his travel writing) resounds with the richness and diversity of the everyday speech of Iranians.

In 1948 the Tudeh was split by a dispute over the party's subservience to the Soviet Union. Al-e Ahmad followed his mentor, Khalil Maleki, an iconoclastic leftist intellectual and social democrat, out of the Tudeh. Though he participated in Maleki's short-lived socialist party, the Third Force, this marked the beginning of the end of Al-e Ahmad's direct engagement in politics. He would return briefly to join Maleki in supporting Prime Minister Dr. Mohammad Mossadegh's 1951 nationalization of Iran's oil industry, but leaving the Tudeh was a turning point in Al-e Ahmad's life, strengthening his identity as a cultural critic and a skeptic, unwilling to adhere unconditionally to any ideology.

By the early '60s Al-e Ahmad was at the height of his power and influence. Following the CIA- and MI6-orchestrated coup d'etat against Mossadegh in 1953, which elevated Shah Mohammad Reza Pahlavi to uncontested power in Iran and brought back the limitations on political freedoms the country had known under his father's rule, Al-e Ahmad renounced politics entirely. To the surprise of many, Al-e Ahmad succumbed to pressure from the regime and published a letter repenting for his participation in the Third Force. Despite his public renunciation, however, it was during this period that Al-e Ahmad unleashed his sharpest and most damaging criticism of the Pahlavi regime.

In response to what he saw as the shah's forceful, top-down efforts to speed Iran's development and industrialization, most importantly through the breaking up of large landed estates and their redistribution to peasants, Al-e Ahmad set out to record the country's disappearing culture. In a series of travelogues, beginning with a report of his family's ancestral village in northern Iran, Al-e Ahmad describes the customs, dialects, history, and habits of these communities, largely untouched by the cultural and economic changes underway in the large cities and towns. His goal in this series was to hold up an authentic Iran to what he derided as the flimsy social order, copied from the West, being imposed by the shah.

Al-e Ahmad's encounter with Iranian rural society also served as the basis for *Gharbzadegi*, the 1962 critique of the Westernization of Iran that was his most enduring work. While *Gharbzadegi* extolled Shia Islam as the foundation of authentic Iranian culture, Al-e Ahmad himself led a secular lifestyle; his rhetorical return to the Islam of his youth was never the wholehearted conversion of a true believer. He continued to drink alcohol and to abstain from prayer. Though he considered Muslim clerics fellow intellectuals, he had little good to say about the religious establishment. And as much as Islam constituted an important aspect of his critique of Westernization, he never transformed it into an all-embracing ideology. His distance from belief comes through in *Lost in the Crowd*, the written record of his 1964 pilgrimage to Mecca. Al-e Ahmad depicts himself as an observer, keenly recording the enthusiasm—and foibles—of his fellow travelers, but he remains detached from them, experiencing the journey as a sociologist, an anthropologist, a political reporter, and a skeptic—but almost never as a pilgrim. In the one moment when he seems overcome by religious emotion—as he prays in the tomb of the Prophet Muhammad in Medina—Al-e Ahmad significantly flees the room, weeping.

In the 1960s Al-e Ahmad traveled widely: to Europe and Israel in 1963; to the Soviet Union and Mecca in 1964; and to America in 1965, where he participated in the Harvard International Summer Seminar directed by Henry Kissinger. Each journey resulted in a travelogue, of which only *Lost in the Crowd* was published during his lifetime. At the time of his death in 1969, Al-e Ahmad was preparing a volume that would collect all four travel pieces under the title *The Four Kaabas*; the Kaaba is the sacred structure in Mecca towards which Muslims pray, the object of the Hajj pilgrimage. The name indicates the importance of these four journeys and how each destination symbolizes one of the poles of Al-e Ahmad's own life: the West (Europe and, differently, America), Communism and the Soviet Union, and Israel. These writings exemplify Al-e Ahmad's eye for detail, his curiosity, and his sense of adventure.

Al-e Ahmad died on September 9, 1969 in his home in a village in the Iranian province of Gilan, most likely from a heart attack. Some, in particular his brother Shams Al-e Ahmad, maintained that he had been assassinated by SAVAK, the shah's secret police. He was survived by his wife, Simin, who passed away in 2012. The couple had no children.

* * *

Al-e Ahmad's interest in the Jewish State began in 1948. In the wake of his break from the Tudeh, he was searching for a non-Stalinist alternative to the Soviet collective farm, known in Russian as the kolkhoz. In the Israeli socialist farming collective, the kibbutz, Al-e Ahmad and his fellow disaffected Communists saw an ideal alternative: socialist but not Stalinist, radical but also firmly rooted in native (Jewish) culture.

Over the next fifteen years, Al-e Ahmad read widely on Israel and Jewish history; he read the transcripts of the Nuremberg trials and the Bible, including the New Testament. He also wrote two stories based on his reading: "The Third Book of Kings," which remains unpublished, and "The Epistle of Paul the Apostle to the Writers," a fictional translation of a "lost" Pauline letter discussing writers' obligations to their society. His interest and publications attracted the attention of the Israeli government, which invited him on an official visit to Israel. On his way back from an extended tour across Europe, he and

and his wife Simin Daneshvar met for a week in Israel in February of 1963.

Al-e Ahmad's trip, as well as those taken by other Iranian intellectuals, can be credited to the work of one young Israeli diplomat. In May of 1961, Zvi Rafiah, twenty-five and on his first post abroad, arrived in Tehran. Rafiah would remain in Iran for only two and a half years, until the winter of 1963. While others at Israeli's semi-official diplomatic mission had established contacts with the military, secret police (SAVAK), the oil industry, and other major sectors of Iranian industry and government, Rafiah was directed to develop contacts with intellectuals, working to increase cultural contacts between the countries. On the Israeli side, he helped bring Israeli performers and artists to Iran and, in parallel, worked to bring their Iranian counterparts to Israel. Rafiah befriended a large circle of Iranian writers, poets, musicians, and thinkers, attending their salons and parties, and began organizing trips to the Jewish State. As many of these intellectuals were already curious about Israel, Rafiah had an easy sell. His own interest in Iran's literature, history, and society—he studied, in Persian, at the University of Tehran, and traveled widely—no doubt helped endear him to culturally patriotic Iranians. The difficulty was not finding enough intellectuals willing to travel to Israel, but finding the money to send all who were interested. "It was a problem of funds," Rafiah told me when we met at his home in Tel Aviv, "I could have brought a whole plane full of artists."

Rafiah arranged official, all-expenses paid trips for, among others, Khalil Maleki, Al-e Ahmad's mentor; Dariush Ashouri, a writer and friend; the painter Hannibal Alkhas, another friend who held an exhibition of his work in Tel Aviv; and the writer Feridun Esfandiary. These travelers' itineraries, Al-e Ahmad's letters from the early '60s and his later writings, as well as Israeli documents on his journey (preserved in the National Archives in Jerusalem), give a sense of the couple's itinerary. These sources testify that Al-e Ahmad and Daneshvar traveled widely, visiting Tel Aviv, Acre, Haifa, and Nazareth. They met writers and poets, participated in an archaeological dig, and Daneshvar gave two lectures at the Hebrew University in Jerusalem. Just a few weeks before the couple was due to arrive in Israel, Rafiah even offered Daneshvar a meeting with Golda Meir, then serving as foreign minister. Daneshvar declined—"What can I say to a world-traveling politician like her?" she protested—but did request to see the kibbutz founded by Israel's first prime minister, David Ben-Gurion.[3]

Simin Daneshvar is a spectral presence in *The Israeli Republic*, mentioned by Al-e Ahmad only a handful of times, and never saying a word. This reflects, perhaps, the tenuousness and tenseness of the couple's relationship on this journey, which came at a moment of crisis in their marriage. While on an extended tour of Europe just before his journey to Israel, Al-e Ahmad had an affair with a young Dutch tour guide. As he explains in his posthumously published memoir *A Stone on a Grave*, Al-e Ahmad was impotent and, following a doctor's recommendation that he provides by way of justification, he hoped that with a younger woman he might be able to have children. Daneshvar learned of the affair from some of Al-e Ahmad's traveling companions just a few days before she was due to leave for Tel Aviv, and responded with a letter telling her husband that she wanted a divorce. Al-e Ahmad was able to persuade her to come on the trip, but the tension between them might help explain Daneshvar's minor role in the text.

* * *

The Israeli Republic is more than a testament to Al-e Ahmad's personal experience. In the early 1960s many Iranian intellectuals were looking abroad, and not just to Israel. One of the key points of the 1962 White Revolution reform program was the breaking up and redistribution of large landed estates, an issue that the Tudeh Party and other left-leaning parties had championed for decades. Finding the ideological rug pulled out from under them, leftist intellectuals were at a loss. Some, who saw an opportunity to work with the government to achieve their policy goals, quickly discovered that the regime was not interested in constructive dialogue. Most dismissed the reforms as a cynical ploy—or even a conspiratorial plot from a regime that they reflexively opposed. As Al-e Ahmad himself wrote some years later in *On the Services and Treasons of the Intellectuals*:

> If the regime pretends to redistribute land, to give workers a share of the profits of factories, and to grant rights to women, it is for the reason that they have kept the real socialists from power and turned their speech into stuttering.[4]

It was in this context that intellectuals turned their attention abroad. On a practical level, they were searching for alternative models of reform that they could advocate without appearing to identify with the government's program. In this light, Al-e Ahmad's—and others'—fascination with the kibbutz takes on special significance. As he writes, his first encounter with the concept of the kibbutz came about after his 1948 break with the Tudeh party. The enduring interest in Israeli collective agriculture among Iranian intellectuals, and the central role it plays in Al-e Ahmad's travelogue, can be attributed to the continued relevance of land reform in Iran. The Israeli government encouraged this interest: visiting Iranian dignitaries, both government officials and others, were invariably taken to a kibbutz, often the same Ayelet HaShahar that Al-e Ahmad and Daneshvar visited.

But a more basic question arose from the dilemma of the White Revolution: what does it mean to be an opposition intellectual at all? Faced with the painful reality of being seen as supporting the government's policies, coupled with regret that they had not stood with Khomeini and his short-lived clerical uprising against the shah in June of 1963, some intellectuals sought to redefine themselves and their role in society. Many chose to ally themselves with the struggles for freedom and self-determination underway in the former colonial capitals of the Third World. Inspired both by the revolutionaries themselves and by *engagée* writers such as Jean-Paul Sartre, Frantz Fanon, and Aimé Césaire (who is quoted in chapter 5), just then being translated into Persian, Iranian intellectuals came to see their opposition to the shah as part of a global movement against colonialism in a new and more sinister form: local elites co-opted to serve the interests of the old colonial masters.

This shift was already beginning around the time of Al-e Ahmad's journey to Israel, but it was only during the second half of the decade that the embrace of Third World struggles became a dominant theme at home. This had serious implications for Iranian intellectuals' general rejection of Israel following the Six-Day War. While military, economic, and trade ties between the two governments continued and even increased in the years after the war, for intellectuals 1967 was a turning point: Israel had become an aggressor and an imperialist power. While, as noted already, Al-e Ahmad's own intentions and allegiances in this travelogue's final chapter are far from certain, the text is testament to the increasing identification of Iranian intellectuals with Third World struggles.

* * *

Al-e Ahmad is adamant, at the opening of this book, about one point: Israel is a velayat—not a country, a state, or some other form of government. But what does this word mean? Velayat in Persian often does mean "country" or "land" and has the general sense of government or rule. However, the word also has a special meaning in Shia Islamic jurisprudence. A *vali* is a guardian, one who manages the affairs of someone who cannot manage them him or herself, such as an orphan or one who is destitute. In referring to Israel as a velayat, Al-e Ahmad is not invoking a general concept of guardianship as opposed to some other form of government. He is envisioning Israel as a *particularly Islamic* kind of ideal polity in which divinely guided leaders—less than prophets but more than politicians—rule.

The concept, which has deeps roots in Shia thought, was taken up by Ayatollah Khomeini and formed the basis for his doctrine of *velayat-e faqih*, the guardianship of the jurist, a foundational principle of the government of the Islamic Republic. According to Khomeini's reinterpretation, in the absence of the Prophet Muhammad and his appointed successors, the twelve imams, leadership of the Islamic community rests on the shoulders of the most senior and knowledgeable clerics; in the aftermath of the 1979 revolution, Khomeini took this role for himself.

Al-e Ahmad's use of velayat does not derive from Khomeini's, even though by the early 1960s the doctrine of velayat-e faqih was circulating among the Ayatollah's inner circle, and the two men met briefly before Khomeini's exile in 1964. However, Al-e Ahmad would not have had to read Khomeini's letters or hear his pronouncements to know that velayat was a term with implications for Islamic politics. At the same time, other Iranian thinkers were developing similar political theologies based on the concept of guardianship as the basis for government.

Al-e Ahmad argues that Israel is a guardianship state because its establishment is a kind of miracle, because it is above the laws and norms that govern the relations of other states, and because it speaks and acts not in the name of the land's native inhabitants, the Palestinians, but in the name of Jews living all over the world. Israel is a velayat, a guardianship state, because it speaks for and protects individuals who are not its citizens. These non-citizens, the Jews of the diaspora, even outnumber the citizens of the state, the physical territory of which, Al-e Ahmad seems to be implying in his discussion of Israel's size, could not even hold all the world's Jews should they decide to move there.

It is not the details of the return of Jews to the Promised Land that are Islamic in Al-e Ahmad's reading of Israel, but rather the priorities of the state and society that they established there: the defense of the faith, exemplified by the capture and trial of Adolf Eichmann; the just redistribution of wealth and agricultural collectives of the kibbutz; the emphasis on universal education, in particular the establishment of Hebrew as the common language; and the effort to reconcile East and West. Moreover, in his visit to Yad Vashem, Al-e Ahmad uses the Persian word *rozeh* to describe the memorial service there, a particularly Shia term for the ritual lamentation for the martyrdom of Hossein, the Prophet's grandson and the third Shia imam, a story commemorated every year with public mourning on the day of Ashura. In Al-e Ahmad's eyes, even in its memorials, Israel is similar to Shia Islam.

In stark contrast, Al-e Ahmad attributes to Arab states such as Egypt and Saudi Arabia perfidiousness, hypocrisy, and greed. Though Al-e Ahmad does not say so explicitly, this same criticism is undoubtedly also directed against the shah's Iran. Lauding Israel as the ideal Islamic state provocatively shows up the decidedly un-Islamic actions of its neighbors. In other writings, particularly *Gharbzadegi*, Al-e Ahmad criticizes the Iran of his day for failing precisely where Israel wins his praise: in education, agriculture, equality, connection to religious roots, and balancing East and West. Al-e Ahmad argues that Israel's presence in the East is a means to return to Islam, a great wind that can sweep away the Arab (and, one can only imagine, Iranian) petro-regimes and waken those who have been lulled into the sleep of ignorance to the call of justice.

* * *

Al-e Ahmad's description of Israel as velayat is provocative and electrifying. Ali Khamenei certainly thought so when he first read Al-e Ahmad's article as a student, and Al-e Ahmad himself, no doubt, knew the strong reaction this metaphor could inspire; he was not above gleefully lobbing rhetorical hand grenades just to see where they would fall. Today it is just as easy to be overwhelmed (and infatuated) by the power of Al-e Ahmad's vision of Israel as an Islamic state: An Iranian who loved Zionism! A Muslim who loved Israel! Encountering these early chapters of *The Israeli Republic* for the first time, it is difficult not to think in exclamation points.

Indeed, the importance of Al-e Ahmad's idea is not to be discounted. *The Israeli Republic* is truly an unprecedented take on Zionism, and, more broadly, in the velayat metaphor, an example of a creative and unexpected way of thinking about Islamic politics in general. Implicit in Al-e Ahmad's discussion is the idea that Shia political concepts are universal and can be applied to explain political formations—such as the Jewish State—that arose independently from the Muslim tradition.

The relevance of *The Israeli Republic*, though, lies elsewhere. Al-e Ahmad's discussion of Israel as the ideal Islamic state marks one extreme of a book that also passes through the opposite position and remains in motion, never coming to rest. *The Israeli Republic* is a portrait in flux. Al-e Ahmad is ultimately unable to decide what he thinks of the Jewish State, and in the final chapter's condemnation are also calls for reconciliation, just as the enthusiasm of the book's beginning is balanced by harsh words; this book falls off the map of the carefully staked pro- and anti-Israel blocs that seem to divide public opinion today. It is because of his ambiguity, despite his occasional hyperbole, that Al-e Ahmad paints a more accurate picture of Israel. Similarly, in his own internal tension, Al-e Ahmad himself is a symbol for contemporary Iran. Both countries contain multitudes and encompass contradiction.

Al-e Ahmad is not the only writer who has trouble making up his mind about the state of Israel; there is more than a bookshelf of Jewish and other writers' arguments and meditations in that vein. This book is important because Al-e Ahmad sees that ambiguity differently, his curiosity drawn to other objects and his reflections informed by other histories. As he writes, "my goal is only that you come to know the disposition, the words, and the 'yes, buts' of a penman from this corner of the world—and a Persian speaker—faced with the reality of the Children of Israel's new country in this corner of the East." Al-e Ahmad's unique perspective is just as fresh, surprising, and challenging today as it was fifty years ago.

The enduring relevance of *The Israeli Republic* does not only lie in what it reveals about Al-e Ahmad's conception of Israel and his character and internal struggles, though, as a preeminent Iranian writer who helped lay the popular groundwork for the Iranian Revolution, that is certainly reason enough. In his thinking about Israel's East and West, Al-e Ahmad hit on a tension at the heart of Israeli society. It would be a stretch to argue that Israel faces a struggle between East and West in precisely the terms that Al-e Ahmad defines, but similar dilemmas have dogged the Jewish State since its conception. Israel was, and nearly fifty years later remains, unresolved about its place in the world and its political and cultural orientation: between Europe and the Middle East, between religion and secularism, and between Judaism and democracy.

The State of Israel was founded in 1948 by pioneering Jewish socialists and cultural revolutionaries, the majority from Eastern Europe, who had come to Palestine to found a modern Hebrew nation. The latent contradiction between the Zionist movement's aspiration to sovereignty for a Jewish majority in the Promised Land—a political vision that included little reflection on the need to protect the rights of the minority—and the state's secular democratic guarantee of equality to all its citizens soon came to the fore. This tension was exacerbated by the war that accompanied Israel's independence, economic hardship, the need to absorb hundreds of thousands of Jewish refugees from Europe and the Arab world, and the Palestinian population, many of whose families had fled or been displaced, and were themselves internal refugees, who had remained, and become Israeli citizens. The strategy of Prime Minister David Ben-Gurion and other Israeli leaders was to consolidate power and punt the problem further down the field. The planned constitution was never written and a series of political compromises resulted in the pre-independence Zionist institutions becoming state organs, and the Jewish rabbinical leadership winning control over personal status issues such as marriage, divorce, and burial. The 1967 Six-Day War and the—ongoing—occupation of Palestinian land, swiftly followed by ideological Jewish settlement, in particular in the biblical heartland of the West Bank known as Judea and Samaria, has only widened the gap between Israel's democratic ideals and its ideological aspirations. Palestinian uprisings, Israel's crushing military responses, and frustrated and interminable peace negotiations have not helped to ease the block. There are now two laws in the territory Israel controls between the Jordan River and the Mediterranean Sea: one for Israeli citizens who are protected by Israeli law, and another for Palestinians—even those nominally ruled by the Palestinian Authority—who are subject to military orders that they have no vote in changing. As one author has presciently articulated the problem, contemporary Israel faces a choice between the goals of ideological commitment and individual freedom, "between those who believe that the earth belongs to the living and those who believe that the living 'belong to the earth'—that it is their duty to make sacrifices to ensure that the land under Israeli control will remain the land of the Jewish people."[5]

Contemporary Iran faces a similar unresolved tension. The 1979 Islamic Revolution ushered in a regime that sought to cure Iran of gharbzadegi, and Ayatollah Khomeini used Al-e Ahmad's catchword often in his speeches.

However, the Islamic Republic, in which ultimate power rests with the clerical supreme leader, is probably not a system Al-e Ahmad would have approved, had he lived to see it; his praise for Islamic government in *The Israeli Republic* notwithstanding, elsewhere in his writings he has little good to say about the clerical class or the legal and juridical aspects of Islam. The Islamic Republic was inaugurated by a nearly unanimous majority in a yes-or-no referendum in March of 1979, just over a month after the final collapse of the shah's regime. Soon, though, as the new government cracked down on left-wing groups, enforced Islamization of the universities and public life, and restricted freedom of the press, opposition to the government grew. Some have argued that had Iraq not attacked in September of 1980, ushering in eight years of costly and brutal war that allowed the leaders of the Islamic Republic to solidify their hold on power, the new regime might not have survived.

In the decades since, and with the selection of Ali Khamenei to the position of supreme leader in 1989, Iran has faced a tug of war within the political elite between those aspiring for internal reform and democratization and an opening to the West, such as former president Mohammad Khatami, and conservatives, exemplified by former president Mahmoud Ahmadinejad, who advocate an ideological hard-line at home and confrontation abroad. In the face of mounting problems, the gulf between the two positions has grown starker: a young and restless population; and the government's loss of legitimacy in the eyes of its citizens after the crackdown that followed the contested 2009 elections. These debates arise from deep tensions in contemporary Iran that can be summed up in the dual inheritance signified in the name Islamic Republic—Islam and Republicanism are not opposed, but these two concepts do draw from different traditions, and conceive of foundational political concepts like liberty, responsibility, society, and law in fundamentally different ways.

In *The Israeli Republic*, Al-e Ahmad saw a tension in the Jewish State between East and West that he recognized in himself. That tension and the ambiguity Al-e Ahmad experienced are still at work in Israel and in Iran today. The continuing significance of *The Israeli Republic* is that it gives the contemporary reader a vantage on the similarities between these internal cultural struggles. In both Israel and Iran unresolved disagreements, born in European Jews' and Iranian Muslims' nearly simultaneous encounters with Western modernity, continue to divide these societies and determine their fates. Al-e Ahmad defined these internal conflicts in terms of East and West, but they could just as well be cast as struggles between tradition and modernity, ideological commitment and individual freedom, or religion and the state. *The Israeli Republic* cannot end the antagonism between Israel and Iran, a war of rhetoric, proxies, and covert operations that has only increased in intensity in recent years. It can, however, indicate how, just as Al-e Ahmad saw Israel through the lens of his own East-West divide, each country tends to view the other through the prism of their internal discord, rather than in terms of rational self-interest. The mutual condemnations issuing from both countries' leaders can serve as an example: in Iran, Khamenei has called Israel "a cancerous tumor in the heart of the Islamic world," and Israeli Prime Minister Benjamin Netanyahu has compared Iran to Nazi Germany and accused the country of "preparing another Holocaust." *The Israeli Republic* can show how, despite this harsh rhetoric, in an important sense Israel and Iran are not in conflict but in concert: both caught in long-simmering internal tensions that are no longer tenable and both, possibly, on the brink of tremendous change.

AMONG THE BELIEVERS

WHAT JALAL AL-E AHMAD THOUGHT IRANIAN ISLAMISM COULD LEARN FROM ZIONISM

BY BERNARD AVISHAI

IN THE EARLY 1960s, Jalal Al-e Ahmad was one of Iran's leading literary celebrities, a writer whose works deeply impressed the dissident clerics who would go on to found and lead the Islamic Republic. Born to a devout family in Tehran in 1923, a boy in the bazaar, Al-e Ahmad had drifted away from the faith and eventually earned a degree in Persian literature. He flirted with the communist Tudeh Party of Iran in the 1940s but broke with it for being too pro-Soviet; then, he helped found (and later left) a workers' party that supported Mohammad Mossadegh, who was elected prime minister of Iran in 1951. After the 1953 coup that toppled Mossadegh, Al-e Ahmad succumbed to pressure from the shah's regime and renounced politics entirely, publishing a letter "repenting" for his prior participation. He returned to his roots and seemed to find his vocation, becoming famous throughout Iran as a novelist, essayist, and underground polemicist, especially for his 1962 book *Gharbzadegi*, or "West-struck-ness" (translated in English as *Occidentosis* or sometimes *Westoxification*).

Gharbzadegi presented the West's technology and individualism—which he saw as little distinguished from its consumer capitalism—as a kind of disease. This sickness, Al-e Ahmad argued, was being spread in Iran by the shah and his old colonial sponsors as they industrialized the country. The disease was all the more insidious for the way it fed on common ambitions—for enrichment, knowledge, and equality—in order to undermine traditional Islamic ways of life based on humility and family cohesion. For Al-e Ahmad, authenticity lay in the village, in rug weaving, in the mosque. "We have been unable to preserve our own historiocultural character in the face of the machine and its fateful onslaught," he wrote.

Among his admirers were Iran's revolutionary clerics, such as Ayatollah Ruhollah Khomeini and his disciple Ali Khamenei (Iran's current supreme leader). Al-e Ahmad was skeptical of the clerics' hierarchy and rigidity, but he thought their preeminence in Iranian society was natural and was pleased that they took *Gharbzadegi* seriously. He shared with them a view of Shiite Islam as carrying the moral prestige of perpetual insurgency: virtue in the face of corrupt materialism, steadfastness against imperial power. Iran could and should import machines, they agreed—piety should not block technology. But as for the freedom of inquiry that produced the technology, that was a different question: if it inevitably brought agnosticism, sexual nonconformity, and greed, then Iran would be better off refusing that part of the bargain.

As Al-e Ahmad's literary reputation grew, so did his eminence and the censors' attention. He made extensive visits to the Soviet Union, Western Europe, and elsewhere, which he chronicled in detail, and even spent the summer of 1965 at Harvard, meeting Henry Kissinger, among other luminaries. He died at age forty-five in 1969, most likely from a heart attack, in his family village in the Iranian province of Gilan. (His brother, Shams Al-e Ahmad, speculated that he had really been assassinated by the SAVAK, the shah's secret police.)

A NOT-SO-DISTANT MIRROR

One of Al-e Ahmad's foreign trips, chronicled in an article and later a book, was to the then-young country of Israel in 1963. It makes for fascinating reading, not least because it is strikingly positive. The travelogue conjures up a long-lost era of calmness and curiosity between Iranians and Israelis, as well as the naive yet potent Third World ideology so common in developing countries at the time. But it is important for what it says, not just for what it represents. It suggests how the Iranian and Israeli leaders who feel such intense mutual hostility today actually mirror one another in certain ways, particularly in their foundational attitudes toward religious authority, political and economic populism, and the West. That a writer such as Al-e Ahmad, guru to the ayatollahs, liked Israel now seems touching. What he liked about Israel seems cautionary.

Al-e Ahmad titled his original essay "Journey to the Land of Israel"; Persian scholar Samuel Thrope has repackaged it in a new translation as *The Israeli Republic*, to evoke "the Islamic Republic." The Iranian visitor was particularly struck by the kibbutzim he visited. He liked their agricultural communitarianism, their pronounced patriotism, their purified retreat from urban ennui—and with tractors, to boot.

In his introductory commentary, Thrope plays up the improbability for all it is worth: "An Iranian who loved Zionism! A Muslim who loved Israel! Encountering these early chapters of *The Israeli Republic* for the first time, it is difficult not to think in exclamation points." But what is more interesting, as Thrope suggests, is how, given the divine socialism Al-e Ahmad hungered for, he was primed to hear Israel's theocratic melody as well as its socialist notes.

Al-e Ahmad saw Israel as a velayat, or "guardianship state"—the sort of polity Khomeini would establish in Iran a decade and a half later. He visited Yad Vashem, the Holocaust memorial, and left in tears, concluding that the new country was an appropriate response to the Jews' tortured history and a useful model for his own oppressed people:

> Israel is the best of all exemplars of how to deal with the West, how with the spiritual force of martyrdom we can milk its industry, demand and take reparations from it and invest its capital in national development, all for the price of a few short days of political dependence, so that we can solidify our new enterprise.

Public education, Hebrew-language instruction, collectivist industry—all these, he felt, would create a new kind of insurrectionary melting pot. Reading Al-e Ahmad, one remembers what few young people can fathom today: how vital, even cool, Labor Zionism seemed back then.

But velayat also had militant religious connotations:

> [David] Ben-Gurion is no less than Enoch, and Moshe Dayan no less than Joab: these new guardians, each one with his own prophecies or—at least—clear vision, built a guardianship state in the land of Palestine and called to it all the Children of Israel, of whom two million live in New York and the other eight million in the rest of the world.

Al-e Ahmad grasped that for Labor Zionists, *avodah*, "labor," was holy in the Tolstoyan sense; he would not have been surprised to learn that avodah means "worship" in the liturgical sense as well. Ben-Gurion, Israel's first prime minister, would have shrugged off such comparisons. He saw Zionism primarily through the tradition of Western proletarian movements, and he and his colleagues spurned rabbinical authority in personal life. Still, he often layered onto his statements a kind of rhetorical messianism ("return" and "ingathering" had double meanings), and he routinely substituted the Hebrew Bible for works of history and archaeology. The Torah provided Labor Zionists with place names and figures of speech. Once the state was founded, and the country was inundated with a million refugees from Arab countries, Israel's leaders increasingly took halakha (religious law) for granted not only as a source of artistic and literary inspiration among free-thinking European Hebraists but as a force for incipient national solidarity.

JEWISH STATE, OR HEBREW REPUBLIC?

There were legal consequences to these ambiguities. The young state's Law of Return and its population registry required a legal definition of "Jew." But what was that?

And who should preside over immigration, the Israeli state apparatus, or the Jewish Agency for Israel, a diaspora organization? As the contradictions piled up in the 1950s, Labor movement leaders and the state's appointed judiciary surrendered to the rabbinical notion that to be recognized as Jewish, one had to have been born of a Jewish mother or converted by an Orthodox rabbi. The designation was not merely honorific. Almost all land available for development, including almost all of that confiscated from Arab refugees, was owned and managed either by the Jewish National Fund or by a state body that, like the JNF, openly discriminated against non-Jews.

Rabbinical courts were given control over marriage, divorce, and burial, as they had been under the British mandate. Civil marriage between Jews and non-Jews was not possible—and still is not. A separate, state-funded religious educational bureaucracy was handed over to religious, and particularly ultra-Orthodox, parties. (Today, more than half of Jewish children in Jerusalem, and a quarter in Israel as a whole, attend the schools this bureaucracy set up.) Ben-Gurion had the parliamentary votes to enact a truly liberal constitution in 1949 but chose to ally with the small religious parties rather than share power with genuine rivals. The original Labor Zionist idea that "Jewish" might be a novel, inclusive national category—might refer to anyone who spoke

Hebrew and lived in the Jewish national home—was effectively abandoned.

Al-e Ahmad repudiated Israel after the 1967 war. But it was in the wake of that war, ironically, that his view of Israel as a velayat would be realized most vividly. Labor leaders now spoke without embarrassment about the miraculous unification of Jerusalem. They sentimentalized the cultural results of deals cut earlier with the Orthodox rabbinate—deals that confirmed Orthodox precepts in ways that would soon lead to the rise of the Likud Party and the eclipse of Labor's more secular and liberal norms. When Prime Minister Benjamin Netanyahu insists today that Israel be recognized as "a Jewish state," Palestinian negotiators may well wonder if he means Jewish in the way that France is French, or a Hebrew republic—or a Jewish velayat such as the one Al-e Ahmad anticipated.

The admiration Al-e Ahmad showed for the Israel he saw in 1963 is one reflection of the confident piety one saw at the founding of the Islamic Republic: the human face of the revolution, some of whose cadres—such as Iran's current president, Hassan Rouhani—the West now hopes might preside over a sort of perestroika. But for Israeli liberals, ironically, Al-e Ahmad's is an embrace they would rather have done without. It is admiration for a compromised democracy that might have been otherwise.

After all, if Al-e Ahmad was right that Israel was a guardianship state, who would be its ideal guardians? Clearly, the Scripture-loving hawks committed to pure collectives and a command economy, to the martyr's version of Jewish history and authentic Jewish rites and law—activists carrying a forlorn hatred for the materialistic, corrupt, and treacherous West and promoting themselves as a vanguard on the Promised Land for world Jewry. In other words, the old Gush Emunim and other zealous West Bank settlers. (One of their number, still unrepentant, assassinated a Labor prime minister.)

So the Israeli forces Al-e Ahmad applauded found their culmination in fanatical rabbis who hate the ayatollahs and are hated in return—radically new Zionists who, as the novelist V. S. Naipaul once wrote of an Iranian cleric, slide down their theology to the confusion of their certainties. Al-e Ahmad's little chronicle is instructive. It is not instructive in the way he intended.

THE ISRAELI REPUBLIC

CHAPTER ONE: INTRODUCTION

THERE ARE TWO reasons I call Israel a guardianship state:

First of all, Jewish rule in the land of Palestine is a guardianship state and not another kind of government. It is the rule of the Children of Israel's new guardians in the Promised Land, not the rule of the inhabitants of Palestine over Palestine. The first contradiction arising from the existence of Israel is this: that a people, a tribe, a religious community, or the surviving remnants of the twelve tribes—whatever designation you prefer—throughout history, traditions, and myths suffered homelessness and exile, and nurtured many dreams in their hearts until they finally settled, in a way, in answer to such hopes and in a land neither especially promising nor "promised." It was thanks, in fact, to the force of time, the necessities of politics, the clear vision of their guardians, or the dictates of economics and unfettered capitalism; I will address each of these in turn.

Now, although one does not dare compare Israel's leaders with Abraham, David, Solomon or Moses—peace be upon them—in any case, today's prominent politicians can be called, if not prophets, then, certainly, guardians, and can be likened to the other one hundred and twenty-four thousand prophets of Israel; of these, we have chosen St. George as the proverbial example of unsuccessful miracles.[1] But this is a true miracle, not some sailor's yarn. Ben-Gurion is no less than Enoch, and Moshe Dayan no less than Joab: these new guardians, each one with his own prophecies or—at least—clear vision, built a guardianship state in the land of Palestine and called to it all the Children of Israel, of whom two million live in New York and the other eight million in the rest of the world. And the most important aspect of the miracle is this: the guardianship state of Israel, with its two million and some inhabitants in that long and narrow land, like it or not, now governs and acts in the name of all the twelve million Jews scattered around the world.

If only one example will suffice, we can call to mind the Eichmann trial. Israeli agents captured him in South America, brought him to Israel, tried him, executed him, and even scattered his ashes at sea—and all this in the name of six million Jews who were slaughtered in the crematoria of a Europe leprous with Fascism, before the establishment of Israel, and on the basis of the policies of a regime whose name, customs, and laws the Germans themselves are ashamed to mention.

This I call a miracle: an event opposed to norm and custom, against international law and the precedent of governments that, even if they sought to fanatically assassinate Trotsky in Mexico with the blow of a terrorist's hammer, at least finished the job on the spot.

If only on account of that example, we cannot but consider Israel a guardianship state, and its leaders guardians: those who march onward in the name of something loftier than human rights declarations. You could say that the spirit of Yahweh is upon them and those prophecies . . . for it was not until Moses had murdered and fled to the wilderness that he had the brand of prophecy upon his breast.[2]

This is the first reason I call Israel a guardianship state.

Secondly, I do so in this sense: the present territory of Israel in no way resembles a country, if by country we refer to the commonly held conception, in other words, something on the order of a continent; the guardianship state of Israel is a small span of earth, approximately the size of the province of Saveh in Iran, less than eight thousand square miles. And how inhospitable! If Moses, peace be upon him, knew to what a rocky place he was leading his people, if he could fathom what a shallow joke the river

Jordan is compared to the Nile, he would never have called it the Promised Land and would not have brought the people for all those years through suffering and hardship.

But in the modern world, numbered among tiny, so-called reputable countries such as Switzerland and Denmark, Iceland and Qatar, Kuwait and the Principality of Monaco, for those of us who are a part of the East this same narrow territory of Israel lies in our arm's reach, like a fist on the table of the Fertile Crescent; it is a source of power and also—on that very account—a source of danger.

Its power or danger depends on your perspective on the world. If your viewpoint is that of the Arab politicians, Israel is a source of danger, preventing the unification of the Islamic Caliphate of which, after the downfall of the Ottoman Empire, so many people have dreamed. But if you look with the eyes of an Easterner like me—devoid of fanaticism and hyperbole and resentment, worrying for the future of an East of which one end is Tel Aviv and the other Tokyo, and knowing that this same East is the grounds of the future events and the hope of a world tired of the West and Westoxification—in the eyes of this Easterner, Israel, with all its faults and all the contradictions concealed in it, is a base of power, a first step, the herald of a future not too far off.

In these two senses I call Israel a guardianship state. In these pages I will attempt to retell what I came to know of it, not for publicity nor as payback for free lunches that I have eaten there; not for the purpose of providing advice to Iran on its two-faced policy regarding Israel, nor to vex the Arabs—my object is not politics; not as a travelogue, nor as a screed. Rather, my goal is only that you come to know the disposition, the words, and the "yes, buts" of a penman from this corner of the world—and a Persian speaker—faced with the reality of the Children of Israel's new country in this corner of the East.

But for transparency's sake and here at the very beginning, I will say that leaving aside tradition and myth and the years of promises and threats, leaving aside what happened before Israel's establishment as a state—all of which is historians' work—from my perspective as an Easterner, the current government of Israel, on the one hand, is the sure bridgehead of Western capitalism, which reappeared in the East in a different form and in other garb following the Second World War. I have grounds for debate with this aspect of Israel. And, on the other hand, Israel is a coarsely realized indemnity for the Fascists' sins in Dachau, Buchenwald, and the other death camps during the war. Pay close attention: that is the West's sin and I, an Easterner, am paying the price. Western man exported the capital for this indemnity, whereas I in the East provided the land: I lack no opinions on this issue either. To put it plainly, Israel is the curtain Christianity drew between itself and the world of Islam in order to prevent me from seeing the real danger; this is exactly what drives the Arabs to distraction.

I also have grounds for debate with the Arabs. It is true that the Palestinian refugees, like a ball chasing the Arab politicians' bat, have with time become accustomed to parasitism. But pay close attention: for more than ten years these same Palestinian refugees have been paying the penance for someone else's sin in that hellish cauldron. From the bones of the Ottoman empire this last piece—this Palestine—that was set aside as a sweet morsel sits like a mace on the table spread between the Persian Gulf and the River Nile. Or is it perhaps like a scarecrow, keeping anyone from extending a hand or foot beyond his own plate?

I will even go a little further: if one day the country of Israel vanishes, who will Arab leaders blame for being the only barrier to Arab unification? Is it not, rather, that the very existence of Israel, and the fear that they have instilled in the Arab heart, is the cause of the modest unity and internal concord of the border guards on this side of the world?

Another point is this: in the Jewish spectacle of martyrdom, the memorialization of the war's murdered and gone, I see the other side of the coin of Fascism and a dependence on the racism which replaced it. But I also say this: If you must be a base, learn from Israel and the high price it has charged! If you are forced to marry one of your distant neighbors, then follow their example! And if your lot is to play the game of democracy, and that too in a land which, as long as there was God, was crushed under the boots of the pharaohs of earth and heaven . . . again, learn from Israel. In any case, for me as an Easterner, Israel is the best of all exemplars of how to deal with the West, how with the spiritual force of martyrdom we can milk its industry, demand and take reparations from it and invest its capital in national development, all for the price of a few short days of political dependence, so that we can solidify our new enterprise.

And this is the last point: the Persian-speaking Eastern-er in particular considers the Jews in a historical perspec-tive. During the ancient reigns of Darius and Xerxes, it was I who sat Esther on the throne, appointed Mordechai to the chancellery, and ordered the rebuilding of the Temple. And although now and then, in the markets and alleys of Ray and Nishapur, at a governor's instigation or for a commander's profit, I have leapt into Jew-killing, nevertheless the tomb of Daniel the Prophet in Susa still performs miracles, and the graves of Mordechai and Esther in Hamadan are no less holy than the shrine of a saint of pure lineage from the Prophet.[3] But leave off laying those obligations and the load of foolish self-satisfaction on the shoulder of God's people. It is enough for me that this very Daniel the Prophet was once my chancellor and I don't care who was his king.

CHAPTER TWO: THE FIRST CALLING

ON ONE OF the hills encircling Jerusalem they have built a memorial, called Yad Vashem (a hand and a name),[4] for all those who died, were murdered, or were cremated in the concentration camps during the Second World War. A huge granite edifice of four walls. Stone blocks from the Jordan valley weighing two or three donkey loads.[5] Each one a devil's marble. A thick one-piece ceiling laid on top of these four walls. A large, rough, black door of leaves of scrap iron. All greatly resembling the tomb of the last victims of Fascism in Rome.[6]

On the day that we went to see the memorial, the man who was our guide delivered a remarkable lament that brought us to tears. But even if he had not been there, and had not lamented so well, we would have cried in any case. What images of humiliation on the walls; what savagery in the man-burning furnaces; what bags made of human skin; what photographs of dark, scrawny men behind bars; and what eyes . . . but, let it be. It is not my goal to deliver an elegy. That same day a Dutch family, in whose honor a ceremony was held, had also come for a visit. Under the broad and hushed vault that resembled a mausoleum, a group of elementary school children sang a hymn, a rabbi prayed, they gave the family medals, and they thanked the father of the family, who during the war had sheltered fifteen or twenty Jews and saved them from Hell.

The person who received the honor was a tradesman, or some such type, with a sort of rough, country face. But in order to be noble, it is not necessary that you be a philosopher or have an aristocratic mien. He must have been a man, of feeling, and compassionate for the fate of God's creation and, able to do so, hid some of the Children of Israel between the crates on a ship and spared them. I mean, so he said in the short speech he gave in response to the round of thanks of the organizers of the ceremony. And he added that, in his own small deed, he had no other goal but to answer the calling he felt in the face of this self-sacrifice, martyrdom, and suffering.

On that day I recalled the passion that called me—or, better to say, us—to Israel on the eve of its foundation, but for a different reason. It began in 1948, or a little after.

We were a group who had split from the Tudeh Party at the end of 1947. As I have written in *On the Services and Treason of Intellectuals*, in looking to justify our actions, we were most industrious investigators of what happened in other similar parties after this kind of split. The Indian Communist Party and, afterward, Tito's cutting of relations with Moscow. Along with a justification, we were also searching for a replacement for the kolkhoz, and in the end we found the kibbutz. There was a shop, and perhaps there still is, on Lalehzar Avenue. It was a textile shop and a tailor's called Melamed. It was also a distributor of Israeli publications and I, at that time, was renting Nader Naderpour's[7] house on Nakissa Alley near Lalehzar. Every day I passed by that store. He put the publications in the display window so that people would see them. Then one day I also saw and bought and read and told Hossein Malek, and things reached such a point that he and I became regular consumers of Israeli newspapers and magazines and pamphlets. It was after that that Hossein Malek published something about the kibbutz.[8] And then the magazine *Science and Life*[9] entered the ring. We together became the transmitters of what reached this country as Israeli agricultural socialism. This reputation led to *Science and Life* being threatened two or three times by the clerics. But we had already found the alternative we wanted to the kolkhoz: the kibbutz. With a socialist framework, but much different than Stalin's brand. After that I saw Koestler's book *Thieves in the Night*, about founding a new kibbutz and the mischief of its Arab neighbors; I came across it because the same author had written *Darkness at Noon*.[10] An account of an experience two hundred times more difficult than our own experience of joining with and separation from Stalin's Nimrodian system. And these were validating and consoling; it was justification. And, inevitably, appealing. Like us, when he broke with Stalin, Koestler was drawn to the kibbutz. Why? Because a base had been established there for socializing the means of agricultural production that had been inspired by Russian social democracy, and not by Stalin. They had planned their work years before Stalin was in power. And, is this not the real reason for the dispute between Israel and Soviet Russia, which absolutely prevents any emigration of Russian Jews?

This was how I came to know Israel. After that, I found the text of the Nuremberg trials and read it, and then I took the measure of the Old Testament anew. I prepared a piece called "The Third Book of Kings" that has still not come out, and something else called "The Letter of Paul the Apostle" that has already been published.[11] After that, I continued gathering and reading news about Israel until February of 1963, when for seven days my wife and I were the guests of the government of Israel. I took this opportunity so that I could tangibly grasp from up close something that until then I had only read about in books, and finally see what had been so appealing.

Aside from this first calling, there were also other attractions.

I, a non-Arab Easterner, have been beaten by the Arabs' stick in the past and I am still taking a beating now.[12] Although I have borne the burden of Islam on my shoulders, and still bear it, they still consider me a "barbarian." They call me a "sectarian." They do not respect Shiites' right to exist. Since their gaze is transfixed by the West and its industry even more than mine, not only do they not really see me at all, but they also regard me as a gadfly. My ports, Bushehr and Bandar Abbas, have been debilitated so that his Kuwait and Basra can be free ports. Since the downfall of the Ottomans until today, the Shatt al-Arab has remained an issue between Iraq and me. The Iranian visitor to the Shiite shrines in Iraq or to Mecca and Medina is ill-treated. In the meanwhile, my Tehran has become a little Paris for every Gulf sheikh's minion who makes a pilgrimage to Mashhad in search of contraband goods; the current rulers of my country have been swindled by this uncouth appearance, thinking that by such dubious hospitality they would pull the rug out from under Nasser's feet in the Persian Gulf. But, after all, this Arab is not an Arab anymore. And yet, for an Iraqi, an

Egyptian, a Syrian or a Kuwaiti, who are certainly not the descendants of the Arabs of the time of the *jahiliya*,[13] before the Prophet's revelation, I am the only one who has still remained a "barbarian." That is, I am the only "barbarian" in the world to these Arabs driving Cadillacs by the shores of the Gulf! All the other "barbarians" have turned into princes and oil magnates. I'm talking about Europeans and Americans. Even Japanese. In this part of the world and for those Arabs, not only do they not have any sign of being "barbarians," but they bring with them the common currency of our day. Hence, Sheikh Shakhbut of Abu Dhabi, and Al Sebah of Kuwait, and the Saudi brood stamp their seal of approval on them, and in place of giving sermons at the grand mosques, their radios blare American jazz and Um Kulthum's wailing. And it is right that it should be so. For the days have passed when I as an Easterner, in the body of the Persian Barmakids[14] and Banu 'Amid[15] and the Banu Muhallab,[16] ran the Muslim world. And in place of our Ja'afari gold,[17] now the dollar and pound rule in the markets of Basra, Baghdad, and the Levant! In this situation, a Kuwaiti is of course right not to notice me, so long as inhabitants of the Persian Gulf, who fled their homelands because of poverty, sickness, and thirst, are willing to hire out their working arms for the hurried construction of his petro-state! And the Iraqi of course is right to block the Shatt al-Arab now and again to the city of Khorramshahr, for the only export from Iraq that comes this way is holy clay used to make prayer stones,[18] equal exactly to the value of the dates we send from Khuzestan. I say all this neither with the goal of inciting a land dispute, nor with the goal of renewing a grudge, nor from a short-sighted political perspective. These are all just heartaches to show the predicament in which, I, an Easterner, and we Easterners as a whole, are caught. In an age when Western Europe alone with the bustle of its common market has even deafened the ear of America, we have been content inside such thick walls, in such close spaces. I, a "barbarian," conclude that I am no longer a barbarian and he, the Arab, concludes that he is no longer Arab. And in the middle of all this, the political leaders of Egypt claim to me that they are the leaders of the Islamic world. To me, who is in their opinion a heretic! And yet, who is this Egyptian Muslim leader? That same one who, after the first blow of Khalid ibn Walid,[19] forgot his own language and culture, and after centuries of being ridden by the Mamluks, now sits on the stone mountains of the pyramids, and has pasted Cleopatra as a lawful replacement for Gina Lollobrigida[20] on the banner of his Westernized literature and press, and, with the spectacle of the works of the pharaohs, begs for alms from tourists from the four corners of the world—and yet, he claims the leadership of Islam! But this Egyptian leader is right as well. For there was a time when I shook a corner of a rug in Abadan[21] and he, four or five years later, propelled by that motion, seized the Suez and accomplished something, thinking that the angel Gabriel was moving his throne. And let us not forget the most authentic of the Arabs, the Saudis, who roll in their oil like pigs grazing in the muck,[22] enjoying it in that very place where the hand of the divine judge set among them the jewel of the Ka'ba fourteen hundred years ago. Of course, this jewel has no more shine now for the Saudi princes, because for thirty or forty years they have been busy at the trough of oil. If there was a day when my pilgrimage and the pilgrimages of Easterners like me provided the cost of living for a year for all the Bedouin of the Hejaz, now it is from the crumbs of the feast of oil that the Saudi progeny fulfill their every desire, and the camels lack nothing either. How could this Saudi, who has no respect even for the Ka'ba, have any respect for me who has been a pilgrim to the Ka'ba? His Ka'ba has been moved to Riyadh and Dhahran, where oil rigs grow from the earth in place of minarets of mosques. And if he still makes a run, it is not a run between Safa and Marwah[23]; it is a run between Aramco and Standard Oil. Or a run between Paris and New York, followed by a whole harem embracing Islam, along with their shameless behavior and their remedies for their hemorrhoids and prostates.

And I, who suffered this way at the hands of these rootless Arabs, am happy with the presence of Israel in the East. With the presence of an Israel that can cut the sheikhs' oil pipeline and plant the seed of the demand for justice and fairness in the heart of every Bedouin Arab, and make all sorts of nuisance and trouble for their lawless, antediluvian governments. The skin that has remained at the foot of the old, but robust tree of Islam in this arid desert—as the remnant of a lizard who lived once upon a time[24]—must be uprooted by the hurricane of the fear of the existence of Israel in order for me, the Easterner, to be able to be freed from the tyranny of the puppet petro-regimes and feel the presence of Islam now crushed under the tracks of American tanks throughout the East. They have transformed its presence into a hidden presence, and without access to publishing tools and news sources, they have forced them to the sleep of the Seven Sleepers of Ephesus. . .[25]

CHAPTER THREE:
A GUARDIANSHIP STATE
WITHOUT EAST AND WEST

BEFORE ARRIVING IN Jerusalem,[26] I did not think any part of it would be under Jewish control. But it was not so. The main nucleus of the city is, of course, in Jordanian hands. Within its high, ancient walls lie the Wailing Wall and the Al-Aqsa mosque. And in its eastern part, the Mount of Olives, that place of Jesus's great revelations.

So it was that from this corner and that market, from on top of a platform or from the roof of a house, Simin and I stretched out our necks until, from afar, we completed our pilgrimage to the shrine of the Dome of the Rock, which faces the southeast, on the edge of a hill facing a valley that meets the Mount of Olives. With the passports in our hands, we would not be allowed to enter there, with its markets and ancient alleyways and mosques. Has any ancient city resigned itself to remain within its nucleus? So why would Jerusalem?

For half an hour we drove through the streets that they built on the hills and slopes on the western side of the city, and everything was new, everything was of local cream-colored stone, until we came to the center of the new city. They showed us on the right side Mount Zion, and underneath it the valley of Gehenna,[27] and then we passed the Knesset[28] and we turned right and stopped by the side of a road. The sun was warm and pleasing. It was a bit past noon and I preferred to stroll. But we had to go to a meeting with an inspector for the Ministry of Education. For lunch. As he had no other time. Lunch was at a table in a cramped and dingy guesthouse, with the smell of onions in the air and a dark stairwell and tiny bathroom, and no sign of fresh food. Again they brought tahini as an appetizer, which I declined. Then a soup that was more or less hot from which, in place of steam, rose the aroma of celery. The Ministry of Education inspector was tall, bespectacled, and knew French better than English. He was of Algerian origin, with dark lips. Like opium addicts. But I did not see him so much as smoke a cigarette. We said our hellos and how-are-yous and other pleasantries, and then he ordered Galilee wine, and in answer to my question as to whether it was from eastern or western Galilee, he said: "Our country has neither east nor west. We only have north and south."

"In a different sense, you only have east and west," I said, "No north and south?"

"It depends on how you look at it," he said.

"Well," I said, "you have crowded this narrow strip of land pretty well."[29]

He thought that I was referring to political questions and their conflict with the Arabs. I got the chills. I made him understand that my point was something else.

"The population of Israel seems to be much more than the statistics you provide," I said.[30]

"This is the third or fourth time that I have heard that opinion," the guide responded. "But why would we give false statistics?"

"In order to calm the Arabs' fears," I said.

The guide and the inspector looked at each other. My wife kicked me under the table to change the subject. I asked: "Am I right that you're a *sabra*?"[31]

A smile blossomed on his narrow face, and he took off his glasses steamed with the celery steam, cleaned them and said: "So you've learned so quickly that you can even give compliments?"

"I didn't know that it was a compliment," I said. "But from your position and from the fact that you know a good local wine . . . "

And the guide added: "It's true."

The inspector was a sabra. But the guide herself was a Belgian immigrant whose husband was lost in the war and with her only child, going from house to house and boat to boat . . . And she had suffered so much hardship until she had finally reached the Promised Land.

Sabras are those whose eyes opened for the first time in this very country, born of immigrant ancestors or Jews remaining from ancient times. One essential difference between sabras and immigrants is that sabras are darker. And they are not pained by the sun. But new immigrants are very troubled by the sun. And they have burned skin. And they always complain about the heat and the dryness. This is the same issue of whether one is or is not accustomed to the environment. The sabra are well named. It is interesting that on account of these immigrants, they have removed the stiffness of the old colonial hat and they have remade it without cardboard and only from cloth, pliable. But its wide round brim keeps the neck in shade down to the hairline.

Then we proceeded to topics that we wanted to learn about from the Ministry of Education inspector. These I will record in brief:

The total population of school-age children throughout the country—in the year of independence (1948)—was one hundred thirty thousand people, from kindergarten to university.[32]

In 1962 that number had reached six hundred thousand. One-fourth of the population. In other words, over the course of thirteen years, education had grown by a factor of five. At this same rate there is a need for classrooms, teachers, and other instructional and educational resources. Inevitably, in the beginning they reached out for anyone they could find, putting both immigrants and sabras in front of the class. Classrooms: from tents and converted huts to spaces under the open skies. And inevitably, before everything else, they have invested in teacher training: an intensive six-month course and in night courses. And in this way, if the percentage of non-specialized teachers in 1952 was five percent, in 1962, they had raised it to one-eighth—in other words, fourteen percent.

The conclusion of our conversation was that perhaps one of the reasons that filling the empty places of trained and experienced teachers was accomplished so quickly was the immigrants' feeling of exile and their need to integrate into society as quickly as possible. In particular if we consider that in addition to classes in formal schools, other classes also exist, mostly at night, for intensive instruction in the Hebrew language, which they have made an official language.

Every newly arrived immigrant learns the language in these classes. As does every soldier (whether man or woman) during his or her military service. These language classes are a first step for integrating the manners and customs of the immigrants, every group of which was uprooted from some corner of the world and came to the

Promised Land. The multitude of nations from which the immigrants are composed are first sifted in these classes. And then in professional associations and guilds and local groups. And this sifting continues until at last we reach two basic groups. These two groups are Easterner and Westerner, even though this is a country "without east and west." But they have poured East and West together in one narrow chalice.

Its people are a simmering stew of the Easterners and Westerners of the world. East and West not in their geographical sense. Rather in their economic sense. A kind of new Haydari and Ne'mati.[33] In a country that knows neither Haydar nor Safdar. With special names, Sephardis and Ashkenazis.

Now I want to leave the inspector of the Ministry of Education sitting at the table and return a bit to history, in order to clarify these two terms.[34]

Perhaps a large number of Ashkenazis are the remaining descendants of a tribe of Khazars living near the Danube who had converted to Judaism.[35] Slowly, they spread out over all of Eastern Europe. The influence of German culture on them was more than any other influence. [Though a number of them still remained nomads.][36] It was among this group that the Yiddish language [a mixture of Hebrew and German and with a relatively rich literature] came into being, and it became the common language of the Jews of Russia, Poland, and Central Europe. In their language this is Ashkenaz [the name of the grandchild of Japheth and the ancestor of the residents of Ashkenaz]. At the same time, there certainly existed in Western Europe as well flourishing groups of Jews with their particular traditions. Especially in the regions of the south of France and the area of Champagne, and they were not related to the Ashkenazi nor to the Sephardi.[37] On the other hand, the Jews of North Africa, the Middle East, and Arabia also have an independent tradition, unconnected to these two groups. Thus it is necessarily an error if we take these two groups to contain all varieties of Judaism. The most we can say is that these two groups are the founders of European Judaism. But the Sephardis ["Spain," in Yiddish] are Jews who lived in Cordoba during the period of the Umayyad Caliphate. In other words, they lived under Muslim rule. When, over the course of a single century, Islam took the Iberian Peninsula with a lightning strike, it provided more appropriate conditions than in other places for the Jews. Perhaps the reason was that their number in the country of Cordoba was larger than in other places. And perhaps also because these Jews' help allowed the Arabs to easily complete that conquest. In any case, during the course of Islamic rule, the Spanish Jews lived in relative comfort [I should add that many of their scholars wrote many books on Islamic thought and culture, just like Averroes, Ahmad ibn Tulun,[38] and even Yaqulun ibn Battuta[39] and Ibn Khaldun[40]. . .]. Even after the

Umayyad Dynasty in Andalus was overthrown, the Jews still held important positions in the courts of the Christian princes, and moreover Spanish historians, as a whole, hold that a large part of current population of the Iberian Peninsula [which is to say today's Spain and Portugal] have Jewish blood in their veins. Especially those who are the offspring of nobles, notables and princes. We know that most of the Spanish Jews and Muslims, after the pressures of the period of the Inquisition, converted to Christianity. But this conversion was only for the sake of appearance. During various stages of the Inquisition, inquisitors eventually became fed up with these false converts to Christianity, those who had remained secretly Jews. This is judged to be the true reason of the expulsion of the entire Jewish community from Spain in the year 1492, the same year that Christopher Columbus discovered America. And the possibility exists that he himself was also of the Jewish race. [Could it be that the illustrious writer is spinning a tale that credits the Jews even for the discovery of America?] It was following this collective exile that the Jews of Spain spread out over the entire Mediterranean basin. Especially in the Balkans. And in particular in the area around Salonika and also throughout the Ottoman Empire, which treated them more kindly than the Christians. These Jews exiled in the Ottoman Muslim empire in some way revived the memory of the time when the Umayyad Caliphate ruled in Cordoba and treated them kindly. And it was this group that retained Spanish as their language for a long time, although they wrote it in Hebrew characters. These are the Sephardim or southern Jews.[41]

You can see that although the first Jews, meaning the first immigrants, who played an essential role in the building of the State of Israel, came mostly from Eastern Europe, in particular from Russia and Poland, the new immigrants have come from countries with a Muslim majority. Hence, two specific strata comprise the current population of Israel.

One has Western culture and manners, because the Jews of Poland and Russia, before coming to Palestine, spent years in Europe, America, or Canada. Take, for example, Chaim Weizmann, the founder of the state of Israel, or David Ben-Gurion, the first Prime Minister.

And the other has Eastern customs and manners. That is, the Yemenites, Iraqis, Egyptians, and North Africans . . . Solving this basic conflict between two types of manners and cultures is the primary difficulty of the state of Israel, which they wish to resolve by means of a common language.

CHAPTER FOUR: THE CORNERSTONE LEFT BURIED UNDER THE FOUNDATION

THE FIRST NIGHT we spent on kibbutz Ayelet HaShahar [meaning "Morning Star"], they took us after dinner to watch the weekly assembly of kibbutz members. It was in a large hall, and about four hundred people were sitting there, women and men, old and young. The men smoking cigarettes and the women knitting. And their eyes were on the performance that was underway on stage, a bare stage with no set. It was a court scene. At the front of the hall, a small space had been cleared and some chairs had been set in a half-circle, facing the audience. This was the judge's bench. A podium on one side and a youth behind it. This was the prosecutor. And a platform, and on it sitting three youths aged sixteen or seventeen. These were the accused.

They spoke Hebrew. But each one in a different way. Sometimes it seemed like Arabic, sometimes like Russian.

And sometimes like nothing I recognized. Later, we had this same experience again, on the night we saw quite a modern stage production of Tolstoy's *War and Peace* in a theatre in Tel Aviv; we really thought that they were speaking Russian. But for the "ha" in place of Arabic "al" at the beginning of words, and the "im" in place of Arabic "un" as the plural marker at the end of words, one would not have thought at all that it was Hebrew. In any case, I asked the translator who was sitting by me and summarizing the essence of the courthouse proceedings. He said:

"We ourselves don't notice it. But to the ears of foreigners, every one of us speaks Hebrew in the accent of that country from which he came. It's a matter of the habit of the vocal cords and the throat and the other organs of speaking. Especially on account of the fact that there is a larger number of those who came from Slavic-speaking environments, their accents are more prevalent."

In any case, the plot concerned those three young kibbutz members who took a tractor one day and, without even having a driver's license, took it on a joyride or for driving practice, and hit the blade of the tractor on a rock and broke it, and now the kibbutz has sustained a significant loss. Now they have put them on trial. Of course, it was a spectacle. Everyone had an opinion as to who the real culprit was.

One thought that the school system and the culture was to blame, for why would a youth who had reached maturity neither have a driver's license nor know how to drive a tractor? And, of course, he recommended a fresh look at the educational curriculum and including more technology.

Another blamed the mischievousness of youth. The safe and secure environment in Israel has taken from young people all opportunity for mischief, but youth must have its mischief at any cost. And if we want to prevent these sorts of things, one must consider other outlets for satisfying young people's need for adventure.

Another held the official in charge of protecting kibbutz property accountable. How could teenagers take a tractor without his knowledge, and where did they find fuel? It's all the fault of bureaucracy and too much paper-pushing; the people responsible for organizing are disorganized.

Now that the spectacle was over, for entertainment between the play and the next meeting's discussion, a man in a military uniform, an officer, came in with a large suitcase under his arm. He went and sat in the place of the accused. He opened the suitcase. Accompanied by the murmuring of couples in the crowd, he poured out the contents of the suitcase on the table. Bullets and mortars and hand grenades, of all sorts. That silenced those present. That fellow started to explain to everyone how to work the different weapons and how to disarm each. Like a military course for exceptional circumstances.

The same day in the afternoon, when we left to stroll on the grounds of the kibbutz, two or three times we encountered cement portals leading underground. We asked and discovered that these were the entrances to underground shelters for the likely war with the Arabs. And where? In kibbutz Ayelet HaShahar, in the western Galilee, where I felt like I did not have the patience for this display of the tools of war. I asked the guide to introduce me to the prosecutor in the spectacle, who was the teacher of the kibbutz school. In the hallway, we made our introductions and set a meeting for the next day and went back to the assembly.

At this stage, they were having a heated debate. Its subject, in brief, was that the kibbutz was no longer able to rely for its income on agriculture alone. At the government's suggestion and given the abundance of labor force along with larger investment capital, different kibbutzim had established for themselves different sorts of industrial, tourism, or educational ventures, in addition to their agricultural foundation. The debate was: What should we do? Should we accept this principle? If we do accept it, then which of these alternative additional paths should we follow? How much capital will that additional venture require and from where will we raise it and how . . . ? (I should add that Ayelet HaShahar itself had at this time its own tourist infrastructure, with a guest house with six or seven rooms, in which we stayed for two days.) We stood to go. My wife wasn't feeling well, so she went to sleep. I went with two members of the kibbutz to the bar in the same tourist hotel, to chat over a glass of beer. We were busy with our discussion of this world and the next, Marxism, Russia, China, and Cuba. It was a while past midnight when two men in civilian clothes with rifles over their shoulders entered and made their greetings. It became clear that they were the kibbutz patrol. They had come to see why the lights were still burning in the restaurant at this time of night.

We had no choice but to stand and say our goodbyes, and the next morning we went to pay a visit to the teacher from the previous night who was the prosecutor in the play. It was a holiday, his wife was at home, and they had brought their child—who was acting terribly spoiled—for a day from the children's house. A four-year-old child. The father was the local teacher and the mother a teacher in the neighboring village, and they had no choice but to send their child to the kibbutz children's house, where they looked over ten or twelve children.

I made a reference to the demonstration of weapons during the previous night's assembly and asked, "How long will it be necessary to motivate people with fear?"

He said: "As long as we are under siege by the Arabs."

I said: "From one of the high officials in your foreign ministry I also heard that you are scared that tomorrow the Arabs will come and cast all the Israelis into the sea. And this is precisely what I am talking about. You yourselves are constantly playing with fire. When you frighten their side you yourselves have to become frightened as well. And in place of eliminating your class differences, you spend your resources building shelters."

He said: "So you tell me, what should we do? We do not want to go to war. But they do not leave us alone."

I said: "It is true that this is your fabled promised land. But do not forget that you took this territory by force and you do not get along with the true owners. I have seen that no one takes care of the villages and cities in the Arab areas. I have seen that they do not even have electricity and schools. You have not considered at all improving the conditions of the Bedouin Arabs in the Negev desert. The Arab neighborhood in Tel Aviv is still a shambles . . ."

He interrupted me: "Do you not know the story of the Arab refugees? They themselves fled. It was because of the war. They committed sabotage. They resisted."

I said: "Very good. You arranged matters in such a way that they were afraid and thought that if they stayed you would squeeze the life out of them. But now the war is over. Do you really not realize that your presence in this area of the world is the cause of the Arabs' pretense of unity? If you could act in such a way that you did not provoke fear or envy, what prop would the Arabs have for their pretended unity?"

And then we moved on to the fact that the kibbutz, the true cornerstone of the house of Israel, is now being buried under the foundation. Then, in reference to the discussions of the previous night that were about looking to add another source of income to the kibbutz, he explained that at the beginning settling in the kibbutz had been a kind of flight from homelessness and a search for stability. And necessarily a return to the land. But now that the state of Israel has been established and the average Israeli has gained a foothold on the land, they feel that state of being uprooted has been stripped away. The average Israeli no longer needs to remain just a farmer. And moreover, every social institution, if it does not progress with time, becomes ossified. It loses its meaning. In fact, little by little people are beginning to say: we will undo the communal life of the kibbutz, which was imposed by the abnormal conditions of first settlement in these lands, and return to a life, the foundation of which is the family. In the days when kibbutzim were first founded—and we mentioned Koestler's *Thieves in the Night*—the residents had a sort of military lifestyle and worked in a barracks environment. But now those days are gone and I am certain that when the Arab threat has passed, the kibbutz will be abolished.

From current events we returned to history.

We are all aware of the importance of the Promised Land for the Jews. In the distant past, the situation was always that an insignificant number of Jews lived in the Promised Land. Others often came there at the end of their lives as part of a spiritual quest and died and were buried there. In recent centuries, however, there have also been considerable immigrations to the Promised Land.

In the sixteenth century, a number of Jews exiled from Spain came and settled. In the seventeenth century, after the attack of the Khmelnytsky Cossacks, a number of Jews returned from Russia to Palestine. And in the eighteenth century, three hundred members of the Hasidim[41] of Russian Poland returned to Palestine. In the nineteenth century, as a result of the ease of sea travel in the Mediterranean, immigration to Palestine increased. Even with all these new arrivals, in the year 1850, there were only eleven thousand Jews in Palestine. In 1880 the number had reached twenty-four thousand persons. Even so, their lifestyle in that land was not so different from everywhere else in the world. The only difference was that they had started the first experiments with living off the land.

But beginning in 1880, the issue took a different shape. Why? The collective expulsions of the Jews from Russia created a new period of persecution that can be compared to the Hitlerian massacres. It was also in Russia that the movement Hibbat Zion was founded with the goal of leading a collective immigration to Palestine and establishing agriculture there.

Had it not been for the financial assistance of Baron Edmond de Rothschild, this initial experiment would never have been successful. It is really appropriate that they gave him the name "the father of Jewish colonization in Palestine." He bought vast estates in Palestine. And he sent many experts and managers to that country. . . and as exile and flight from Russian continued, new groups of people were arriving constantly, which was how the oldest Jewish colonies in Palestine were established in Rehovot and Hadera . . .

After the failure of the 1905 revolution in Russia and the renewed persecution and expulsion that followed for the Jews, a large number of the Jews of Russia, and the majority with a Tolstoyan ideology, came to Palestine in order to work the land by the strength of their arms and the sweat of their brows. These were the founders of the first kibbutzim. These were the first agricultural collectives that are among the rocks of the state of Israel. It was under these conditions that the Zionist movement was ripening among the Jews of the world. The movement of these Russian emigrants in Palestine coincided with the establishment of the Jewish National Fund in 1904 by the world Zionist movement, the goal of which was to encourage the colonization of lands in Palestine . . .

It was in this vein that in 1909 the city of Tel Aviv, which began as a small settlement in the northern environs of Jaffa, was established. In 1914, although the colonization of the lands had still not expanded, its roots and foundations had been fixed. The First World War was a difficult experience for the Jews of Palestine. Their number decreased from eighty-five thousand to sixty-thousand individuals. But their German, Dutch, Scandinavian, and American brothers rushed to their aid and for the first time they became concerned for the fate of the Jews in Palestine.

During the period of the war, the Jews established the Jewish Legion that served in Allenby's army in Egypt. It was thereby that on the second of November, 1917 Weizmann received that famous promise from Lord Balfour: that the Jews have the right to build their national home in Palestine. On the tenth of December of that same year, Allenby's troops entered Jerusalem. And the entirety of Palestine was conquered in 1918 (which was supposedly under Ottoman control). By the mandate of the League of Nations, the British became the protectorate of that area. A new movement of immigrants began immediately after the First World War. Stronger than earlier movements. For various reasons, it continued until the Second World War.

The new immigrants came, first of all, from Russia and then from Poland and finally from Germany, where the Hitlerian persecutions and tortures had begun. The population of Tel Aviv, in a matter of a few years, rose from forty-thousand individuals to one hundred sixty-seven thousand.

It was at this time that the conflict began between Arab and Jew which has still not subsided. Not only did the British postpone fulfilling their promise, but day by day they became more aware of the Arabs' opposition, continually inflamed by Colonel Lawrence. Following their own well-known policies—divide and conquer—the British had preoccupied the Jews and Arabs in Palestine with conflict. And they prevented immigration. We must not forget the massacre of Jews by Hitler, in addition to the obstacles that the British placed on permitting entry to Jewish immigrants' ships. Over and over, it happened that immigrants' ships wandered from port to port until they were able to release their passengers.

From 1939 the difficulties for immigrants increased . . . and with the end of the war, the conflict between Jews and Arabs in Palestine reached its ultimate height. It would have been easily possible in the period between 1918 and 1948 to reach a reasonable solution for the conflict. A number of Jews, including well-known individuals like Martin Buber, supported a single Jewish-Arab state. And it was not the case that personal relations between Arabs and Jews were entirely rancorous everywhere. But in order to reach a solution, it must be desired and sought after. The English wanted something else. It was on this account that they neglected every appropriate chance for reconciliation, on purpose, until the time when the English announced that they would abandon the mandate in Palestine.

In 1947, the United Nations prepared a plan for the partition of Palestine that pleased neither side, neither the Arabs who opposed any partition, nor the Jews who thought that the strip of land which was their share was too narrow . . . when in May 1948 the English took their forces out of Palestine.

CHAPTER FIVE:
THE BEGINNING OF DISGUST[43]

And now I think that my heart of steel
Would change color,
Rusting in the blood of my brothers
So innocently, so unjustly slain.[44]

This text is a friend's letter from Paris to which I have added
a thing or two of my own. The nonsense and beard-pulling is
mine; the reasonable speech his.

—JALAL AL-E AHMAD

For two weeks now, my ear has been glued to the radio
and my eyes to the newspapers. I am writing to tell you
now about my heartache that resulted from this tour of
"European philosophy." Only during acute political and

social crises can one find the true import of words and statements, actions and movements. It is only at critical moments that the true potential of every faction and every individual becomes apparent, and it is only when they are cornered that one can accurately discern the true nature of the friendly and enemy forces. And this is exactly what happened with respect to the recent war in the Middle East: their true identity was revealed and their true nature branded on their foreheads; even a letter of regret will not take the shame away. What racists and what Arab haters are the French, small and large, the left along with the right! No one thought—and I least of all—that the imprint of Algeria would remain on their hearts like this. The misadventure of the invasion of the Suez Canal in 1956 and their failure inflamed them to seek revenge. In the words of Aimé Césaire, "All of these animals of various colors are belligerent troops of colonialism. They are all slave traders and they are all debtors to the revolution."

It took two whole weeks to "shape public opinion." And then, who first leaped to the field of battle? The leftists! The gentlemen of global conscience—those who in their own decayed minds think that their "mission" is to defend the rights of the whole world. Those who condemn Peter and Paul, or whomever they wish in the most remote corners of the world in the name of "humanity!" They fell over each other to reach the battlefield. From Sartre (and he less than the others) to the Rhinoceros, the pig known as Eugene Ionesco—whose shamelessness has reached so far that he claimed, "the stateless Palestinian refugees, who for twenty years have been residing in war refugee camps and who receive from the United Nations rations amounting to half of an average person's daily caloric intake, all want to finish the work that Hitler left undone." Meaning that they want to massacre these assorted European and American Jews who are the representatives of Western culture in the middle of the Arab countries! Another lunatic by the name of Claude Lanzmann, who is a member of Sartre's *Les Temps Modernes*, became so enraged by the imaginary savagery of the Arabs that he directed everything that he could pull out of his sick mind at these people. The Left Federation[45] and the honorable Mendès France[46] are of the same type, but even worse. But most shameless and most heinous of all was Daniel Mayer,[47] who is the head of the Human Rights League! And in the name of the historical mission which is conferred on him, he laid his egg as follows: "I abhor my Socialism [!!], I abhor my humanity, but I take pride in my Jewishness."

In the period of a single week, this became the state of these literary and political rascals; and what a circus! You should have been here! But after their angry foaming at the mouth, then the real bosses, who pull the strings, entered the pit. The field was ready. The French Left (excluding the

Communists, who themselves do not realize what the hell they are doing!) had all together prepared the sentiments for their next fishing expedition. The bourgeois press and the organs of money and profit were lifted on the shoulders of these so-called leftist intellectuals! The signing up of volunteers began and money started to be collected. His excellency Baron Edmond de Rothschild, the general secretary of the supporters of Israel in hysterical anti-Arab racist rallies—took his place at the side of the most famous elements of the Left. All rushed together to the aid of civilized Israel in its war against the backward and savage Arabs. In order that you understand and not take my words as exaggeration, I will give you just one example. It is five months now that a committee by the name of the "Billion Francs for Vietnam Movement" has been active, the goal of which is evident from its name, and which until now has only collected twenty million francs. But in the span of forty-eight hours the amount of money collected for Israel in France passed three billion francs! Only half of which the family of Rothschild, of Paris and London, donated.[48] And you yourself can read the expanded version of the story between the lines of this summary.

Well, why are these humanitarians making such a great effort? Why did they display this unified front with Israel? The answer is simple: for twenty years, a bunch of bullies, with the aid of international capital and with the blessing of Zionist terrorist organizations and the Hagana,[49] has occupied Palestinian land and forced out a million of its inhabitants. For twenty years they have been seizing Arab land bit by calculated bit. For twenty years the United Nations has been asking them to allow the Palestinian refugees to return to their homeland and they reject them like roughnecks. Over the course of this time, they have been condemned for aggression exactly eleven times by the United Nations. And three times they have clearly invaded the territory of neighboring countries, and not once have they accepted the Arabs living in Palestine as Israelis. This is the reason that now Western humanitarians have stood in their defense, all at once and as one body. The Nazis' behavior yesterday towards the Jews is what the Jews, with the aid of the troubled consciences in Europe and America, are, as we speak, doing to the Arabs.

Because Nazism—the cream of Western bourgeois civilization—poured six million ill-fated Jews into those man-cooking furnaces, today, with the support of Wall Street capitalists and the Rothschild Bank, two or three million Arabs from Palestine, Gaza, and West Jordan[50] must be killed and become homeless. While the illustrious European intellectuals were accomplices in Hitler's crimes, and at that hour did not say a word in protest, now they have given those same Jews a bridgehead in the Middle East so that the nations of Egypt, Syria, Algeria, and

Iraq can be scourged, and so that they will not nurture a thought of struggling against Western colonialism in their heads, and they can never again close the Suez Canal to the civilized nations! I spit on their stinking bourgeois civilization! I wonder at those gentlemen, who for years drummed into our ears that Israel is a socialist country: Are they really sleeping restfully these nights? The same Israel that as the Middle Eastern branch of imperialism and the CIA now directs all the anti-revolutionary spy networks in that region? The same Israel that has even chosen its name as a smirk to the Palestinians? Is the fact that the head of the Egyptian government's relations with our government are estranged a reason for sacrificing one hundred and some million Arabs on this issue? Now Iran gives ninety percent of Israel's oil and the Iranian government, out of its fear of the Arabs, declares, "Regarding the company, we have no authority. They themselves sell oil to whomever they wish!" And is this excuse not worse than the sin itself? After all, are we supposed to be duped by this blatant lie, or that the aid of the Red Lion and Sun Society[51] to the refugees in Jordan which, even in the most dire political conditions, never goes beyond public deception? The fleeing Arab soldiers in the Sinai desert are dying in groups from thirst while the whole Persian press is full of vengeance against Nasser, and no one writes that it is these civilized Israeli gentlemen who have cut the water pipes so that they won't have too many expenses in holding the captives! Moshe Dayan returned from Vietnam just six months ago, where he had gone as an intern to observe how the so-called civilized Americans are massacring the hungry, savage people of Vietnam with napalm, fire bombs and flamethrowers! But so be it.

The lash of events is more jolting than any exhortation or sermon. The French press, which like the other media institutions of this country is in the hands of Jewish capitalists, has poisoned and stupefied the people's minds to an extreme, the likes of which will not be seen for many years to come. And of course, the private and state radios operate with their advertising money. Is it not the case that the French prime minister is the head of the Rothschild bank?[52] That the guiding reins of Hachette and Renault are in the hands of capitalists? That the entire flank of the Left is in the powerful hand of Guy Mollet,[53] the same man who sent the army on an expedition in the Suez? And that their propaganda is in the hands of those who still dream of "French Algeria"? This is not strange; what's strange is that it is those very men who also construct the conscience of the Iranian intellectuals. These days I am disgusted at my knowledge of Persian. In the whole Persian press, aside from one article in *White and Black* magazine,[54] I saw nothing else that could be said to be written by an Iranian. If the conscience of European intellectuals is troubled by having consented to Jew-killing, what is the excuse of the Iranian intellectual whose queen was Esther and Morde-chai his minister to the Achamenid kings! And for whom the tomb of Prophet Daniel was a sacred shrine? The con-science of the Iranian intellectual should be troubled by the fact that Iranian oil burns in the tanks and planes that are killing his Arab and Muslim brothers. The conscience of the Iranian intellectual must be troubled by the fact that Saudi and Kuwaiti oil burns in the tanks and helicopters that constantly attack the poor people of Vietnam with their bombs. Who said that the foreign press must shape the conscience of the Iranian intellectual? And the luna-cy of Rothschild and Lanzmann? It is an outmoded notion that we in the Middle East must pay the indemnity for a madman's sin committed in Germany and Europe. The matter is this: does Israel—this direct puppet of capitalism and Western colonialism in the Middle East—which has so much capital, not know that the oil company bought ev-ery date palm for a thousand tomans in Kharq?[55] If Israel wants to live peacefully in the Middle East, it must not be a center for the conspiracies of anti-democratic movements.

If Israel wants our Arab brothers to recognize it offi-cially, instead of acting as the salt sprinkled on an open wound, it must be a salve administered on the pains of the Middle East, the greatest of which are colonial influence and oil plunder.

Now let me quickly decipher for you the riddles of the events of these last few days, for I have seen what the censor does with the Persian press, and I know that you do not really know anything about this issue. For I have seen that today's Persian press looks as if it was actually published in Tel Aviv.

On Monday, at six in the morning Paris time, Israeli planes, with the aid of American and British planes, which took off from Malta and bases in Libya (and for this reason Libya threatened to close them), bombed all the airfields of Egypt, Syria, Jordan, and even Iraq, and Egyptian organizations announced that, of these bombed airfields, one was even on the Egyptian-Sudanese border, had not been completed, and was only known to exist by Egyptian government officials and American officials! Then a deceptive maneuver took place, when the Israeli forces bombed the American ship *Liberty*, which was not able to receive information about the movement of planes, that is, which direction they were going.[56] In this way the Arab air forces were disabled on the ground in the first hours, and the result was apparent from the very beginning. Then the tank battle began. The Sinai desert was captured in two days. Under heavy Israeli bombardment, six hundred tanks and seven Egyptian brigades were disintegrated. For they had no air defense. The number of dead, between seven and ten thousand people. More important even than these are the ten or fifteen thousand who are now wandering around in the Sinai desert and are dying from thirst—as I have mentioned—while the conquering Israeli army refuses even to take them prisoner, because if they do so they must give them bread, water, beds, and tents. The Jewish people are frugal, of course. We know this from long ago. Perhaps, they will give them only a mass grave!

But on the Jordanian front, under Israeli bombardment, the Jordanians were not able to resist for more than three days. And they put fourteen thousand dead in the ground. The civilized Jews seized all the area of West Jordan, and now they are forcing another million Arabs from their homes. It is interesting that at the same time that the Israeli press and radio (to which I have listened closely) present the war as a religious war between Muslim fanatics and civilized Israelis, the entire Israeli cabinet and army officers are weeping and lamenting at the foot of Jerusalem's Wailing Wall. At that very same time, Radio Cairo incited the class of revolutionary workers to take up arms and defend against the colonizers. Not only were all the political prisoners in Cairo released, they were armed and set off to the defense. But the Israelis did not cross the Suez Canal, though they could have. For they did not want to give an excuse to the colonialists for having become the cause of the closing of the canal. In any case, on Wednesday, to the whole world's astonishment and surprise, Egypt announced that it accepted the Security Council's ceasefire directive, and the next day Gamal Abdel Nasser, in his half-hour speech, stated that he was resigning from all his responsibilities. (And I have the impression that not even the smallest mention of this speech has been published in the Persian press!) The announcer on Radio Cairo was not able to read the news of Nasser's resignation to the end and began sobbing, and the civilized Europeans still had not recovered from the shock of this news when in the Arab countries there was an uproar, and in the space of half an hour, according to Israel Radio (I am writing precisely): five hundred thousand people in Cairo poured into the streets, demanding that Nasser's resignation be withdrawn. Again, according to Israel Radio, from the shores of the Atlantic Ocean to the Persian Gulf, in the space of a few moments the distress of defeat turned into a resolve to return Nasser to office, such that all forgot that they were at war and that they had lost. An hour later, Nasser stated that he would withdraw his resignation until the following day so that the parliament could decide what he should do. But the next day, Nasser was not able to go to the parliament. From his house to the parliament a sea of men had closed the road to any kind of movement and passage, as could be seen on television. The likes of that kind of demonstration can only be seen in Beijing. During this time, the diplomatic ties of all the Arab states with America and England were cut. The Suez Canal was closed. The oil faucets of all the Arab countries were shut. Once the military defeat of the Arab forces was confirmed, and the thought of the humanitarians and cultured elites was soothed on this account, in the whole of France the radio and newspaper and television all turned to the oil issue. Will the matter become serious and the West be left without oil? This is what I gathered from the statements of the French publishing mills concerning the oil issue: the French nation could sleep peacefully knowing that America and England were cut off from oil, but not for themselves, adding that the oil of the Middle East is the cheapest oil in the world and Iranian oil (which everyone is talking about), the cheapest in the Middle East, and that this oil is open to all. For its replacement, the local officials of the companies have even set rewards, so that every organization will be more active; and moreover, in addition to us, there are also the Americans who without Iranian and Persian Gulf oil would not able to endure one moment in Vietnam. (I do not know if it has also been reported there or not that in Saigon people so rushed to the gas stations that two pumps were broken!) Secondly this: that the oil of the region of the Gulf is seven times cheaper than Algerian oil, ten times cheaper than oil from the region of Panama, and twenty times cheaper than American oil; if the Americans had to get the oil to Vietnam themselves, their war budget would increase fivefold. Necessarily, their economy would collapse. So, thank God that Iran still has oil and has promised to increase the extraction of its oil so that it will compensate for the shortage of Arab oil. This is precisely the same thing that the Kuwaitis did when our oil was nationalized. Yes, this is the biggest token of the solidarity with our Muslim brothers, that both in those years and now, ends up only in the interest of the civilized Europeans, Jews, and Americans!

This is all true. But still the task has not been completed. On the Syrian front, the war continues. Radio Damascus says that the war is not finished but rather has been postponed. They are sending all the women and children from Damascus to Lebanon and from Cairo to other areas. Fortifications are being built in front of every house, every building, and every administration office. The entire population, with the exception of the disabled, has been armed, and Arab radio stations are propagandizing that even if we are defeated on the front, we will turn the war into a guerrilla war. As I see it, the situation is taking the form of a new Crusader war. But this is a war that is no longer motivated by religious conviction. Rather, satiety and hunger are its motives. But that is between the Christian nations and Muslim nations. The leader of the Christian nations in this war is colonialism and the leader of the Muslim nations is anti-colonialism!

And if in those wars the European Crusaders lost, they succeeded nonetheless in winning the Islamic world's science and art, and this time, with the help of that very science and art, and with the help of a big brother, international colonialism, and a little novice, Zionism, they have returned to fight that same war. Is it possible that the Muslim nations of the world in this new war will take back what they gave the West in the previous one? In any case, so be it. Let me continue with the news.

Abdel Nasser in his address said: "On the very night of the fourth of June when the Israeli attack began, American and Soviet representatives recommended that I take no steps to attack and assured me that in this way Israel would also not attack, and the issue would be solved diplomatically." And then he added: "We were waiting for an Israeli attack from the east and north, but we found ourselves under attack from the west"—there are important air bases in Libya that are under the exclusive authority of the American army, but Nasser did not name them explicitly—and he said that the CIA had doubtlessly been involved in this incident. And such things.

But the latest news is that Egypt's losses in the war (apart from the loss of life) are estimated at five hundred million to one billion dollars. China has sent a sum of ten million dollars in cash and one hundred fifty thousand tons of wheat as emergency relief. From the night of Nasser's resignation until now, the Soviet embassies in Arab states are under police protection. For the people of the Arab states are enraged by the Soviets' lack of censure—they dictated a ceasefire with the agreement of the Americans—and their lameness. Though this is once again the same bitter experience, repeated a hundred times: taking a wife but counting on the neighbor's virility. But it is not clear how the Soviets are able to recover from this shame. As, apparently, the Supreme Soviet of the leaders of the Eastern European communist parties had an emergency meeting and severed all of their relations with Israel; but still, cutting relations is one thing, while the hopes of the Arabs for direct aid is something else!

Houari Boumediene[57] did not accept the ceasefire. You know that he went to Moscow so that, as part of the most progressive wing of Arab rule, he could clarify the relationship of the Arab governments with that former "laborers' headquarters." And for this same reason the European liberal (!) press soured on the fire ignited by this former revolutionary soldier. For they still believe that zeal and ardor are found among the leaders of the workers, but they have made a mistake. The most extreme action would be another declaration. But declarations have never improved anyone's condition. I have heard that Kosygin[58] said to Tito[59] (through Tito, Nasser had requested immediate aid from the Russians): "Do they think we will run to the canal in order to sacrifice ourselves for the Egyptians? (And he was right; those gentlemen did not dare to take a step even in Vietnam.) We have given them weapons; if they have the will, then let them make the move!" This is the response to the request for aid. It means that the Sinai desert is a new laboratory for testing weapons. And the more important embarrassment is this: that the Soviet weapons have lost their reputation as reliable. And the reputation of American, French, and English weapons has increased.

In any case, this war has dire consequences. The Israelis have explicitly declared that the past will not repeat itself, that not only will they not return the occupied territories but also that they will expel those territories' Arab residents, which they have already begun doing. The Russians are trying hard to make others accept that they are serious, and as for the Americans and English, the situation is all to their heart's desire, but there is no doubt that in the Arab world a deep transformation has taken place. A whip has struck the backs of the ancient sleepers, the result of which will soon become clear. If, that is, the ruling administrators of the Arab governments, most of whom are instruments directly controlled by the oil companies, are capable of keeping the oil faucet shut. Palestinians throughout the territories occupied by Israel have reconstituted resistance committees and, according to the representatives to the United Nations who have come from there, are planting the land with Chinese mines. Woe be the day that sees Chinese feet treading again on this region! Of course, you've also heard the news of their hydrogen bomb. The basic problem is this: that I fear Israel, with this bullying and becoming the policeman of the Middle East (a traveler said that in New York, with its three million Jews, in the days of the incident, such an environment of terror has been created by the Jews that all are in retreat!), will incite a new movement against the Jews. If you want the truth, it is Zionism that is dangerous, for it is the other side of the coin of Nazism and Fascism. It works in the same way. For me, the Hagana is no different than the units of the SS. The Socialist André Philip[60] had written that it is shameful that here in France a number of the Jews have written and stated that their homeland is Israel, not France, and I see it as sorrowful that the French press is in the hands of the Jews. (*L'Express*, with its Servan-Schreiber,[61] who is their mouthpiece and that of the whole chain of the press; the Lazareffs[62] with *France Soir*, *Elle*, *Match*, *Paris Match* and others . . .) In addition to the fact that Jews manage all the television transmitters in New York (thirteen networks), and most of the publishing houses and newspapers.

It is true that the difference between Israel and the Arabs is the difference between the twentieth century and prehistory. An Israeli who has immigrated from Europe or America is a man of the technology of this century, while a Middle Eastern Arab is still an idol-worshiping builder of pyramids. An Israeli has a per capita income of one thousand dollars a year, and an Arab, eight-seven dollars. Is it not horrifying that the daily expenses of the Palestinian refugees are between eight and eleven cents? Necessarily, the Israeli wins. But who has kept the Arab back in the period of constructing the pyramids? Anyone other than the colonizer? Anyone other than the company? And anyone other than its agents and supporters? And the experience of Cuba and Algeria and China has shown that the hand of colonialism can only be severed with an ax, and not with promises and threats and oaths and agreements and human principles and humanitarianism! This is a certain fact that Middle Eastern Arabs have also understood. Here is the danger. Hence, long live the gendarmes guarding the oil pipelines! I am so frustrated by Nasser that I don't know what to say. You, who want to go to war with King Hussein and the Saudi prince; don't you know that you have made a mistake? Don't you know that by setting your hopes on the governments of Kuwait and Qatar you can't get anywhere? The interesting thing is that the Saudi representative to the United Nations is a Lebanese Christian, a lackey who does their bidding in order to double his wages. At the same time, America's representative Arthur Goldberg[63] is a Jew. To grasp at such a frayed rope in the pit of war, again in the unrealistic hope of emergency aid from the "laborers' headquarters"—taking such a risk— indeed such a lesson had to be the consequence! Have the Arabs awakened?

The interesting thing is that these so-called respected gentlemen, the leftist intellectuals of this country, con- stantly throw the stone of Israel's civil measures and ad- vances at the Arabs' heads. And they conclude, therefore, that the Arabs do not have the competence that the Israe- lis do. But no one tells them: Dear sirs, consider Kuwait, which until yesterday was a barren desert and now with the aid of oil capital has become the Arab heaven; and then consider the royal gardens in the Saudi capital Ri- yadh, where at the foot of every tree an air conditioner is blowing cool air on the trunks of the trees; the debate is not over who has the competence and who doesn't. The debate is over the fact that anywhere you make a large in- vestment, every precious rarity from chicken's milk to hu- man life is available.[64] The only thing is that the chicken's milk is for the Israelis and human life, for now, is being taken from the Arabs.

Of course, you will ask: fine, but according to you, what is to be done? It's very simple. Nasser and the others, who in pursuit of a ridiculous demagoguery constantly speak about pushing Israel into the sea, are talking nonsense. The only solution to the problem is forming a federal government of Arabs and Jews called Palestine. The same thing that the Jewish philosopher Martin Buber proposed years before the establishment of the state of Israel. Otherwise, I see that the gentlemen from the two sides are sharpening their bayonets! Zionism is exactly as dangerous as the Arab puppet governments. Israel must divorce its fate from Zionism, and Egypt, Algeria and Syria must divorce their fates from the Arab petro-states.

Finally, we here are trying to gather medicine for those wounded in the war. Is it possible for you to do the same there? The government of Iran is making a show in Jordan that apparently no one has taken seriously. For it is hidden from no one what kind of aid it is, and that its goal is to bury vengeance. A step must be taken by the people. After all, in addition to all these problems, we are supposedly dealing with Islamic cooperation and solidarity.

NOTES ON SELECTED CORRESPONDENCE

BY SAMUEL THROPE

AT THE END of September 1962, Jalal Al-e Ahmad left
Tehran for Europe on a UNESCO-funded fellowship.
After participating in a meeting of education publishers in Paris at the beginning of October, he remained in
Europe for four months, traveling to Germany, Switzerland, the Netherlands, and the United Kingdom, before
departing for Tel Aviv at the beginning of February. Al-e
Ahmad participated in conferences and workshops, met
old friends and fellow Persian writers who had found refuge in Europe from the political climate in Iran, and dis-
cussed his own work with local academics.

Throughout his travels, as during earlier and later pe-
riods they spent apart, Al-e Ahmad and Simin Daneshvar wrote letters. Beginning on the day of his arrival, Al-e
Ahmad wrote home almost daily, and Daneshvar's letters

to him from Tehran were just as frequent. While not all the letters reached their destinations (both Al-e Ahmad and Daneshvar regularly complained that the other was not writing), this massive correspondence is a testament to the depth of their relationship. In the version published in Iran, edited by Masoud Jafari Jazi in 2006, their letters from this time take up nearly 350 pages.

In this translation, I have selected the letters that are the most relevant to Al-e Ahmad and Daneshvar's trip to Israel. This correspondence sheds light on their plans and expectations for that journey, and adds significantly to the scanty information that Al-e Ahmad's travelogue provides. The letters also demonstrate the close ties between the couple and the Israeli diplomats, particularly Zvi Rafiah and the ambassador Meir Ezri, living in Tehran. Not only do Daneshvar's letters mention phone conversations with Rafiah to discuss the details of their trip, but she also met the diplomats socially, at a lecture organized by Khalil Maleki, Al-e Ahmad's political mentor and friend.

However, even in these letters most focused on Israel, other issues come to the fore. Many of the letters are taken up with the details of everyday life that are the basic stuff of a marriage, even at a distance. Al-e Ahmad writes often about his lack of money, his fascination with Europe, and his fantasy that he and Daneshvar could leave Iran, with which he had become so disenchanted, to settle in Paris or London. Though Daneshvar had already published two well-received collections of short stories (*The Quenched Fire* in 1948 and *A City Like Paradise* in 1961), she was occupied for most of the 1960s with her teaching responsibilities at the University of Tehran, leaving little time for writing. Alongside reflections on the events of the day, including the volatile political situation, her letters record her many obligations: to family, to the university, to friends, and to her husband. The letters also reflect her loneliness and sadness, feelings compounded by the revelations of Al-e Ahmad's infidelity.

In this correspondence, it is, in fact, Daneshvar's voice that comes to the fore. Her presence in the travelogue is minor, fleeting. Al-e Ahmad never depicts her as speaking or records what she might have said, instead deploying her as a comic sidekick and a silent foil to his own lively and impolitic self. The letters show how much is missing from this depiction. In practical terms, Daneshvar participated actively in their Israel journey, speaking with women's groups, giving lectures at the Hebrew University, and taking part in an archaeological dig, among other activities. Reading her letters, it is impossible not to take heed of her powerful, independent voice, and it is difficult to imagine that she would have been as restrained as he makes her out to be. The letters fill in that missing piece.

Al-e Ahmad and Daneshvar refer to numerous friends, family members, and acquaintances. I have followed Professor Jafari Jazi's annotated index to his edition, which identifies many of these figures. In a few other instances, I have identified them on my own.

As already noted, this is a small selection of Al-e Ahmad and Daneshvar's voluminous correspondence. Other letters, which provide more detail about some of the events and characters mentioned but are not immediately relevant to their Israel journey, have been left out. To the extent possible, I have provided some of the missing context in the notes, and I hope readers will be forgiving of what is necessarily an incomplete text.

SELECTED CORRESPONDENCE
BETWEEN JALAL AL-E AHMAD AND
SIMIN DANESHVAR, 1962–1963

MORNING, FRIDAY, DECEMBER 14, 1962

MY DEAREST JALAL,

It has been exactly seven days since I've had news from you and my heart is terribly distressed, though I didn't show it and wrote nothing important in Wednesday's letter. But I know that as soon as I talk about it, it will lose its power.[1] You asked what I'm going through in your absence? It's clear what is happening, but what is the use of disturbing you there in foreign lands with commentary on my mental states, which you know are fleeting. Now that you have a chance to see the world and experience it—for better and for worse—I keep pricking a needle over and over in the same terrible place. And you haven't once brought it up. What's more, you know me, if anyone does. Normally, I keep my cool and can preserve my calm (though with difficulty). Do you remember when my mother was sick and almost no one could tell from my appearance what was truly going on inside me, in my heart? Now, though, I don't have control over myself to the same degree. Partly because the years have taken their toll on me, and then also partly because of your departure at such a moment, which I consented to while clinging to a hope that I've written of time and again: that your morale will improve, that you will come back and lift my spirits in turn. That's all. Of course there are hours when I want to head out to the wilderness, and hours when I'm calm, but little by little I've become resigned and content, and the truth is that it's for the best that you haven't been here these last few months while I've gotten myself back under control. Because you're not to blame for marrying a wife who is heir to a portion of strange sorrows. In any case, fortunately it has passed, but along the way I wanted to test my powers of endurance, and I'll also say this: sadness makes a person grow, because it is by tasting sadness, not happiness, that a person discovers compassion. The "happy-ending" Americans are the only truly happy nation, who seek out dangerous experiences just to experience the taste of sadness.

I think that's enough. Now I feel perfectly fine. This afternoon is the annual memorial for your father, which

I'm going to at two o'clock. May God bless his soul. But you want the news.

First of all, congratulations on your Israel efforts working out, and on the Jews inviting you for a week. Since you've been gone my relationship with Rafiah[2] (whom both of us thought was Rafia) has not languished. I sent one of my students, who had written an essay about the sources of important Bible stories (only four stories), to him, and Rafiah really helped him, and sent me an illustrated book. I called to thank him. To get to the point, I was a bit sly and spoke about your idea and even said that he should send me, too. Yesterday morning he called back and said that he had managed with Jalal's trip but that my going presents headaches that are difficult to resolve (the same problems that prevented Minister of Education Derakhshesh[3] from going). In short, now when you go to London you have to go to the Israeli embassy and they will take care of the rest of the process (for a one-week stay), though of course, being from the nation of the Children of Israel, they skimped a little on the ticket. By the way, before you go to London write a letter to Rafiah and send him your exact address. This adds a week to our time apart, but it doesn't matter; you dreamed of seeing that place and now you have a good opportunity. If I've already waited four months, I can wait another week.

A letter from Parsa came with yours. He is now engaged to a pleasant, thin European woman. Unfortunately, he didn't write his correct address on the back of the envelope. Otherwise I would have sent the copies of *Gharbzadegi* to him, not to Mahmudi. I have Mahmudi's address—the Iranian embassy in London—and in my view it's not a good idea to send such a book there. Now I'm trying to find a suitable address. Otherwise, there was a letter from Baqerzadeh, who kindly sent his condolences. You will probably see Parsa in London. It's not worth sending him a letter. Last night Mrs. Jadali[4] called and said that once again his letters are not arriving. I instructed her to write a letter now to the Dutch address, which she didn't have. I wrote it for her in clear handwriting and sent it with her chauffeur. Because of your father's memorial, which the men commemorated last Thursday in the mosque, Shams did not come this Wednesday. I will see him this evening. I've also spoken with Dariush[5] on the telephone. I sent your greetings and he sends his. Sohrab Dustdar was also supposed to come today, but he sent his apologies instead. The weather is rainy and lazy people generally do not leave their houses on such days. Otherwise what news can I share? As for *Der Spiegel* newspaper, it has caused quite a commotion here.[6] We wanted to take advantage of it, too, but nothing happened. Partially due to laziness, mine and others', and partially due to the belief that the whole affair is rather frivolous. A package of propaganda books, in German, came yesterday with your letter, which I kept apart from your books. I have no hope that the photo books of Chinese and Japanese art will reach me. The post office must have kept them for themselves. You don't know what bazaar thieves they are. It's not like over there, where if you leave your bag in a taxi, it turns up two days later. If you only knew how distressed I was when I read that you had lost your bag. But you should know that I always cheat: I read the end of your letters first so I can see whether my letter arrived, and whether any potential problems have been resolved or not. That way, my distress doesn't last too long. So as soon as the subject of the bag came up I read the end of the letter. I'll leave the rest for later. I have nothing else to say for now.

11:30 A.M., MONDAY, DECEMBER 18, 1962. ON THE DELFT–AMSTERDAM TRAIN

MY DARLING SIMIN,

It'll be good if I can write you something on this train. This morning when our guide came, she had brought not only my check and others' money, but also two more valuable "checks": letters from you. From December 7 and 9. Thank you. They came exactly to the right place at precisely the right time. More essential than the money they gave us. And the money is 425 guilders, which they also call florins, as you know. And I'm going to cash this check tomorrow. And in exchange for all this money, our program in Holland only lasts until next Friday. Because you know that the Christmas holidays start on Saturday, December 22, and we have nothing to do here but wait around uselessly. I suggested to my fellow travelers that we go to London instead of coming to this country and spending money uselessly. If we can, we'll go. This morning in Delft, which is a center for technical colleges, we were welcomed by the mayor at a reception in the city hall—where it is said that their aged queen's funeral was held recently. Mayors here are appointed by the superstitious queen and her fortune-tellers, but under the mayor are four people elected by the populace, and one of the four, who was the official in charge of culture and health, spoke with us afterward and was the first person on our itinerary. In any case, since I have an appointment this afternoon in Amsterdam, now I'm sitting on the Delft–Amsterdam train. But back to answering your letters. Because I want to send this letter today.

First of all, your letter had an air of loneliness and unhappiness they've never had before. Until now you had kept yourself from expressing your true feelings in your letters, but this time they came screaming out. How nice it would be if you could come to London. Wouldn't it be possible to take a month of leave? It would be so good, really. Then we would go together to Israel. Think about it, and look into it. Use the money you've saved for the ticket and come. You know how happy it would make me. Seriously, think about it. I can't bear the thought of you unhappy or crying because of my absence. I'll wait for you to take the first step.

You had written about Derakhshesh and Shams's promises to him. Please explain to him that, whether he likes it or not, I've become his advocate here and in places he can't even imagine.[7] (The train is swaying terribly, but I want to mail this letter today. Forgive the slanted and crooked handwriting.)

I've also written you about the fog and smoke in London. But you should know that my turn to kick the bucket hasn't come yet. As for Dariush, one can't just go along with whatever he wants, and the more I thought about it, the more I asked myself: what can I write to his daughter? I don't know the language of children in general, let alone the language of spoiled and cutesy children. We couldn't find a compromise with Dariush ourselves, and the stupid boy sees that you are alone, and at the same time he complains to you about his relationship with Farough, etc.[8] It's all nonsense. And you're not obligated to carry the weight of his unreasonableness. In your place, I would keep him at more of a distance. If your loneliness didn't torment you so much, you could avoid seeing him entirely. (Now we are stopped in the station in Leiden so my handwriting is better). Regarding your bourgeois upbringing,[9] etc., Dariush was also talking nonsense. We had an honorable upbringing, or the upbringing of honorable people, and others don't understand what we're doing or what we're saying. I gave Jadali the two lines you wrote about him for him to read.[10] He felt better. I had supposed that his wife hasn't sent any letters because she's ill. Thank you for calming the man's mind. May God grant you a long life! You bring both of us joy with your letters. (The train is moving again.) I also don't need the support of the Communists, with their discussion and criticism sessions, and never needed it. Let a dog piss on their graves. I'm not the kind of son of a donkey whose saddle gets crooked because of a comment from Radio Moscow.[11] We say what we have to say, and anyone who wants to can enjoy it, and those who don't, don't. Anyway, you have my London address. But how nice it would be if instead of sending money you came yourself. It would be an unexpected gift.

Well, those are the answers to your questions. But about this place: it is the kingdom of canals. When we were in Delft, all the streets had a canal running through the middle with lots of bridges and trees on both sides. How pretty it was. But can I enjoy it? My eyes don't notice beauty anymore. Without you the world is empty and ugly and dull. And just as we have gutters and dikes and aqueducts for bringing water to the land, here they have twice as many gutters, canals, and dikes for removing water from the land. This country is one big drain from end to end. Otherwise, today was sunny. With our arrival, the weather improved; sometimes there are wisps of clouds, but the weather is good, humid, and healthy, and not too cold. Last night I slept well, too. Our itinerary in this country is not too packed. If going earlier to London isn't possible, I will try to find Siyar,[12] perhaps where we're going in Amsterdam, and spend my days off with him. The good thing about this country is that it's small and we're only staying in one hotel. It's easy to start out in the morning, go anywhere, and return to The Hague in the evening to sleep. I learned that The Hague is by the North Sea, and as soon as I arrive, if I have a chance, I will go to the seashore. In any case, from now on I'll be happy because I can get my letters directly at the hotel. And that's enough for now. The train is moving again and shaking a lot. Bye bye.

9 P.M., DECEMBER 18, 1962

DEAR JALAL,

Now, my dear, you have become a distinguished man and a good boy. I'm in such good spirits this week that I don't know what to say. I received a wonderful letter from you. A long and plentiful letter and a postcard from Berlin, a letter from Hamburg, and a package of books from Siegburg, including a *Red Book* for Shams. Yesterday morning I sent you a letter from Tajrish[13] and I went to the bank and took out 500 toman. Now we have 1,500 toman in the bank. I'm telling you this because there has been no difference in our expenses in your absence. And now I understand that you, my dear, didn't have any expenses. Like a swallow, you were apparently eating only air. The main reason for taking out money, in short, was to give money to your mother, because they have had so many expenses in preparation for your father's annual memorial. I also only gave her 400 toman for the memorial, not 600 toman. It was a mistake. Now I don't know who accepted all this money, but I believe that your mother gives away most of the money that you give her (I'm guessing). Shams also helped of course.

In any case, after the bank I came home and showered, and then at noon went to Mrs. Qudsi's[14] house on Shapur

Road near the Mokhtari market. (What a big mistake, according to you!) The whole family was gathered there. I gave Shams the book that Dustdar[15] had intended for him, and gave 150 toman to your mother. And I came back home and read your letter again. I called Mrs. Jadali and told her to write a letter so she could put it with mine, so she can reach her husband through you. I sent it. By the way, yesterday Rafiah called and said that you must not forget to go to the Israeli embassy in London, and he asked me what kind of interests you have so that they can make arrangements for you accordingly. I said, "If you send me to Jalal, that would be best; he's very interested in wild animals like me!" What I actually said was: the opera, the theatre, the kibbutz (I don't know if I've spelled it correctly or not), a few contemporary writers, and a synagogue and its services. He said, "We don't have a proper opera, but we'll keep the rest in mind." By the way, how can I tell Naraghi, who calls every day (and has tasted the publication of *Fashandak* on his tongue), to republish one of your works, like *Awrazan*, which is out of print, instead of a second monograph?[16] Write me with the answer. A nice photograph also arrived, my thick-mustached ragamuffin. You won't get rid of that patched overcoat? I'm giving it to the junk man when you come home. Oh, I'm annoyed you don't buy anything for yourself. What am I going to do with you? Living only for your brain and heart. Tomorrow night Shams, Islam,[17] Mohasses,[18] Shahrashoob Amirshahi[19] (the wife of Hezarkhani[20]), and Latifa will be here. Shams has invited them. I didn't say a word. Let the boy figure out the consequences for himself.

Good night for now. I have to fill the hot-water bottle and go sleep all alone in the cold room upstairs. That hot-water bottle has been a husband in many respects, even when you were here, but now it has a place all its own. I miss you. I hope to see you in my dreams. I often dream of you.

SIMIN

4:45 P.M., MONDAY DECEMBER 24, 1962. AMSTERDAM

DEAR SIMIN,

From now on my life in Holland is my own. Let the devil take the itinerary . . . I mean, if I was in The Hague that's how it would be. That's why I escaped and came here. They called from The Hague again this morning and reminded me about the event on December 27, which is here in Amsterdam, and that there is no sign of a letter. I have asked them to send your letter to me here as soon as it arrives. I don't think that a letter will come by tomorrow, but I'll hang on to this letter until the day after. How is your mood and how are your days? Does the wood stove work, and do you light it with me in mind, and do you sit by it alone? You have firewood. I hope that I actually fixed it when we rebuilt it in the summer with Taqi the junkie. Really, send my regards to everyone. They are all poor, or helpless. But about my days:

Last night I got into bed at eleven, but I didn't fall asleep until twelve. I read the Gospel. This, too, is one of those hotels where they put the Gospel in the rooms. Throughout Europe there is a crusade to put at least one copy of the Gospel in every hotel room. And I've seen hotels like this from Switzerland on. In France there was no sign of such things. In Switzerland there was. In Germany there was. Here, too. And the association that published this book, which includes the entire Gospel of Luke and the first chapter of the Gospel of John, has announced on the back cover that by 1960 it had placed copies in twenty thousand hotel rooms. If I can, I'll take one. It's in four languages: French, English, German, and Italian, and it's helpful to compare the texts. Today I was flipping through it, because I don't have any other books to read aside from Hafez and the Quran, and those hold no novelty for me. Jadali also has a selection from the *Masnavi*[21] that we enjoy reading together sometimes. Anyway, I slept until 8:30 a.m. and then, like an elderly gentleman, I shaved and trimmed my mustache and ate breakfast and went with Jadali to see a private museum that is perhaps the phoniest and smallest I have seen in Europe so far: the museum of the Holy Land and the areas where the Semitic religions, Judaism and Christianity, originated.[22] It will be useful if I end up in Israel. Even though it was only two rooms, it had two mummies and two interesting replicas of the Tabernacle and Solomon's and Herod's Temples, including the current state of the Temple that has become the Dome of the Rock and the Al-Aqsa Mosque, and Omar's Mosque, etc.; it was useful. And then we walked back by the mansions along the dikes of the upper city. On a thirteenth-floor restaurant that towers over all of Amsterdam, we sat and had a coffee and watched the city for an hour, and the strong sun made it sparkling and splendid, and then we left and went to the market to find me a good overcoat. A *demi-saison* that also has a wool lining and opens and closes with a zipper. Believe me when I say that in all of Amsterdam (we looked on three streets) they didn't have one, and kept asking us to take their spurious goods off their hands, which I badly resisted—meaning, I resisted well. (Now it's five o'clock and the windows are dark, and the room is so well heated and nice that I shut off the radiators.) Then we bought bread, cheese, butter, and fruit for dinner for the next two or three days, and came to the hotel and ate lunch, and then went to our rooms. I prepared tea with hot water from the sink; I also have tea and sugar, though Jadali drinks all of it, so we have divided it in half. And I peeled an apple and then drank the tea and swallowed a vitamin C pill with the doctor's medicine, and got in bed. I slept until four. Then I got up, cleaned my face and Jadali came, wanting to go out. I told him I wasn't going. The truth is that it was terribly cold outside. Between fifteen and twenty-five degrees, and this raincoat can't handle such cold anymore. The truth is that if it weren't for the cold today, I would never have gone looking for an overcoat. Because the hotel is so nice and warm I imagined that everywhere would be the same, and when I left this morning I didn't put on my camel-hair coat and went out wearing just this same black suit, and now my throat hurts. . . It's terribly cold. You can't understand how cold, no matter what I say. I've never seen such a chill. Our guide in the boat yesterday said that if the cold continues this way for two more days, all the canals will freeze over. And you know that Amsterdam has seven hundred canals, and all its business flows through them.

Okay, my darling, that's enough. I will try to rest these few days in Amsterdam. All the better because it's cold outside and I have more opportunity to stay at home and rest. I need it. Because I know that when I get to London I'll have a whole new itinerary.

FRIDAY, JANUARY 11, 1962

JALAL MY LOVE, MY DEAR,

Last week I had three letters from you. I'd like to ask that this nice tradition continue: keep writing three letters a week. Two of your airmail letters , which you had written from Thursday, January 2 to Monday, January 5, came together on Wednesday, but I'm surprised that, of all the letters I've written you, you've only received two. I've consistently written three letters a week, and also sent *Gharbzadegi* and *Arash*[23] to this same address at the British Council. One airmail package containing four copies of *Gharbzadegi* and one copy of *Arash*, and another package with copies of *Gharbzadegi* by ship. My guess is they must have been handed out as alms to the poor souls in the post office, because now that I'm looking at a calendar I see that I sent the airmail package on Wednesday, January 4. In short, the mail has gotten lost for any number of reasons. One is that it's January, and another is the terrible cold that has frequently delayed flights. Golriz Siyar[24] telephoned and made small talk; she is waiting for her flight to Amsterdam to take off. You had written about Farzad[25] and Golchin Gilani.[26] You were right about them. You also wrote about the film *Barabbas*.[27] Dariush's book has been published, but has still not been distributed. You can do something to help. Amir Kabir Publishers is in

London and its address is at the same British Council. You can take the initiative and take the money for publishing *The School Principal*[28] from them. But listen to the report of your little one's last few days.

I had a class Wednesday evening and then I mailed your letter. Maleki[29] had invited me to his house to meet the English socialist, and quite the Jewess, Maria Saran[30]—though of course he had not explained what the real story was—and I went (because of all the trouble I had given them Monday morning).[31] I met her, God bless. Nearly two hundred people—women and men, big and small, family and strangers, limping and crippled and healthy and strong, old and young and little girls—were lounging in all the rooms of the house. Of all types and races and ideologies—from Dariush Farouhar[32] to Dr. Said Fatemi,[33] from Mrs. Bamdad to Mrs. Dolatdad, and Maleki's disciples. You could say I was quite surprised, and I stationed myself next to Mrs. Dolatdad. An old woman of seventy-five with white hair, two humps, and red, squinting eyes entered, and Maleki ran the *cours* toward me, and, before I realized what was happening and could get out of the way, he was introducing me to this woman, who is the secretary of the women's party of the International Socialist Organization, there to give a lecture, and saying that poor me was to be her translator. Believe me, I was so mad that if I had stabbed myself, I wouldn't have drawn blood. I had no inkling that something like that would happen, and teaching for three hours had made me tired, but in any case I translated and brought it to a swift conclusion in good humor. Then Reza Maleki[34] invited me to Café Fard in Tajrish and insisted that we come, and so Parviz Maleki[35] and I went together. They hosted a long dinner, telling jokes and clinking their glasses. Of course, the Israelis were also there, meaning Rafiah and the head of their mission, Ezri.[36] Rafiah sends his regards and said that it's strange they didn't provide you with an itinerary in London. Everything is taken care of and we all decided that you should write to him; I sent you the address through Shams and perhaps by now you have written him something. By the way, Maleki also stepped in and suggested that I go. He has now become convinced that I should. Rafiah said, "Get your passport and the authorization and we will get you a visa." That's why I didn't refuse. I said I'd think about it. In addition, their offer came after Maleki's intervention, and they only invited me because they know that there is no way I can go.

Anyway, that night I got back home at midnight. Thursday morning I went to the city and serviced the car and spent the evening at Vicky's[37] house. She had a dinner—you were missed for the turkey *pulao* and pomegranate and walnut stew. Leila[38] is also better and Anush[39] was invited, too. Khosrow suddenly said, "Dear Simin, congratulations!

Look at you translating at this socialist gathering!" He gave a whole report on the evening. It was clear that he had heard about it from Hooshang Tale,[40] who had referred his beloved friend for military service. I said, "If I drink water in this town, everyone hears about it."

But I woke up late today. Now the kids are playing badminton in the yard and I'm writing. This morning Vaziri[41] called and thanked me for the classes. Last week I taught for nine hours, five for my own lessons and four for Vaziri. I also wrote a letter to you. The weather here is good, but this year there has been no proper rain. It is cold and dry and sometimes there is frigid sunshine. What else can I write? You know, now that your arrival is imminent, I miss you even more. Last night I dreamed of you. I dreamed that I had to wait another four months, and in the dream I cried so much that Ali woke me up and said, "Auntie, what happened?" But it's always the opposite of a woman's dream that comes true, and there are only twenty-five more days until you come. I also straightened the house and have almost nothing else to do apart from waiting. My darling, fatten yourself up so that you can fatten me. Have mercy for your long, dark, stupid Simin. Truly stupid. Why do I pretend that everything is normal? But regarding the trip to Israel I almost refused, because I didn't want Maleki, or even you, to intervene on my behalf. I want to be invited on my own merit.

11:00 A.M., WEDNESDAY, JANUARY 16, 1962

DEAR JALAL,

Again, this week I have had no news from you since Friday. On Friday evening your letter arrived, and I answered it. Are you going to Israel? How are you? Of course, yesterday Vicky called to say that a letter had arrived from you, and I'm sure I'll also receive one today—at least somewhat sure. And I know that two or three letters will arrive together. You had written in Vicky's letter that you appreciate your black wife. Am I black or are you? Oh patience stone doll![42] All of a sudden that came out of my pen. Although sometimes you really are the most patient of men—other times the most impatient. But Vicky called in the afternoon to say that your letter had come. I went all the way to the city to read it. I wasn't smart enough to tell her to read it to me over the phone. They were happy you had written them. But regarding Parviz Farjam,[43] a good egg and so far my only consolation in your absence, his employment is being sorted out, meaning he has found another job so he has no need for us to build a school or dig a well and steal a minaret.[44] Boy, this grunt work of teaching and education. It doesn't suit either of us.

But you'll want the news. I wrote you that at Maleki's house one night I translated that English woman's speech into Persian. That same night he grabbed Rafiah and his boss, insisting, "Boys, send Simin to Israel, too!" They half promised to do so. Yesterday Rafiah called saying, "If you'll go, we'll send an invitation." Since I would see you a week earlier, I can't stop thinking about accepting the invitation. If I meet you halfway, it would seem as if I came all that way just to greet you, and on top of that, we would have a weeklong honeymoon together. Parviz Farjam has also promised to take care of my passport, but I'm still unsure. I'm afraid to go there without you having come back yet. Perhaps you've entirely given up on the idea of going, and anyway I'll be a bother and a nuisance to you with my gabbing. Of course I don't know if official permission has come from their center or not. By the way, Rafiah blamed you for his late apology and his inaction. He said, "Jalal never told me to invite his wife. Any time there was a conversation about it he said, 'I want to go to Israel.'" Of course I was a bit upset by that. He was trying to say that he didn't have permission from my husband to send his wife, in which case I leave it up to you. First of all, tell me: should I come or not? Secondly, tell me clearly: what date and time are you arriving in Tel Aviv? Also, I don't know anything about Israel. My knowledge is limited to Ashouri's[45] travelogue in *Kitab-e Mah* and an essay by one of my students about four chapters of the Torah. But I sent your letter on Monday. That same day I gave the carpets to be cleaned since they're so full of dust. Parviz Dariush called in the evening to invite me over on Thursday (tomorrow) at noon, but Mohin Afifi, the previous wife of Abbas Daneshvar,[46] had already invited me to lunch and I had accepted. Monday evening I prepared my lessons. Yesterday morning I went shopping (what a luxury a car is). Then for the love of reading your letter I went to Vicky's again in the evening and stayed with her until 8:30 p.m.

This morning I took a shower and washed my hair and braided it. This evening I also have three full hours of classes. I had written you in earlier letters that Leila is sick. Now she's better. Don't be worried, if you were. Anyway, I'm thinking about the moment when you come, and I will escape from this drawn-out loneliness and my flowers will bloom all at once. Listen to the stupid thing I did. Yesterday I sat like one of those barbers who, when they don't have work, shave each other's heads: I read my last journal entries and made myself cry over what Islam calls my bad luck. It's a strange artist who makes herself cry this way. Anyway, I haven't decided when I'm going to see your mother. I think I'll go Friday, or at the latest Sunday at noon and ruin their lunch.

Now three crows have come and are walking in the yard, so at ease and comfortable you would think that they inherited our house from their fathers and grandfathers. The filthy dogs don't even talk to each other. Each one is walking along its own path. You watch the pigeons and talk about the pigeons, and I watch the crows. Sadly, despite the fact that all the housework is done and the house is ready to receive you, my love, the gardens are not yet in order. I'm waiting for Mustafa, who has perhaps been deceived by the land-reform proposals; I don't think he will come here anymore. No laborers come to the city at all anymore, nor does anything else. The farmers are so full of hot air, you have to come and see. His Highness puts on a show of socialism and everyone believes it. Obviously with American approval. If you start shaking out the rug, you'll find American advisers are in all the key positions—the army, education, planning and budget—the news is everywhere that Mrs. Lambton[47] is coming to Iran. Yesterday, when I was coming back from Vicky's house, I turned on the radio and listened to His Highness's speech. Now they have announced a referendum on the six-point reform. I don't think even Lenin gave such promises to his people. On that same day we encountered a roadblock in our path at the shah Abdol Azim shrine: buses of the farmers who had come on pilgrimage to Reza Shah's tomb.[48] Last night on Vicky's television I saw them interview six of the farmers. One (a former peasant of the Bayat family from Arak) said, "We've produced so much dairy to send to the masters in Tehran that we're sick of the smell of yogurt and butter and oil." Then we ourselves went and bought a stinky garlic cheese from the coffee shop to spread on our bread. I know that in the end Arsanjani[49] will be booted out, and I know that it's all bogus and superficial.

YOURS,

SIMIN

10:00 A.M., MONDAY, JANUARY 21, 1963. LONDON

DEAREST SIMIN,

Today is the first day of the month of Bahman. They gave me your letter when I went to breakfast this morning, and I read it as I ate, and now I'm reading it again and will answer it piece by piece. First of all, regarding Israel, I've written you about the letter I sent to Rafi'a. Secondly, if I make the time today or tomorrow—and I will—I'm going to make a reservation. Though the PEN Club is supposed to throw a party during the last days of the month—after the twenty-eighth—it has no impact on my plans and in any case I'm not staying in this city a day later than the end of January. Can you believe that I haven't yet seen one-third of the city, haven't yet gone to one-third of the museums, etc.? It's too cold and I'm too busy with nonsense. In any event, in my next letter you'll know what day I'm leaving and when I will arrive in the Israeli guardianship state. Rahnema's letter still hasn't arrived informing me what happened and what he has done, but you should absolutely get ready for Israel. How could you be a nuisance? Our companionship is worth the whole world to me. Really, tell me what's happening to you? Why don't you send letters? Who made you so angry that you're barking at me? Your last letter gave off a strong odor of politics. I mean, it smells like the political fever in the country is terribly high. Only God knows when it will be sweated out. And around here there is not even the smallest symptom of that fever, not at all. It seems that no one takes it seriously. And what's certain is that I, too, believe that the teetering egg has broken. Whatever happens, happens. Regarding Arsanjani, don't be troubled. For now the real donkey's ass has calculated that this charitable land reform will make him beloved by the people. . . (Now the woman has come in and is making the bed, and I can't concentrate on what I'm writing.)

Otherwise, I have no plans this morning. I think I'll go do a little more shopping. After 10:30 a.m. we have an event at the British Council, where I'll be until evening. Regarding the letter from Vicky and Parviz, you know that I really like them, and I feel that they need terse, serious words sometimes. That's why I wrote something for them. If they didn't take it badly, all the better. Your older sister's experience is so present that you're unable to let others, those who are the closest to you, feel even a little discomfort, so that they won't talk about it and not be trapped by it, and you can complain, "What does it have to do with me?"[50] Let them find their own way. Of course, Vicky was a real bully from day one. That's why I'm not worried. You understand what I'm talking about. Well, that's enough for now. I'm not obligated to use up the whole piece of paper. I'll bring it to the post office. That's better. And then I'm going to arrange my airplane tickets and do a little shopping and afterward the event, etc. Send my regards to everybody. Especially to Dariush and Shams and both families and my mother and everybody. Jalal is waiting to see you in Tel Aviv. Did you know that in Arabic, Tel Aviv is "Tel Habib"? Meaning Lover's Hill! Can it be that we will see each other there?

YOURS,

JALAL

The truth is that because of you these colonialist London publishers will perhaps take something from us. Meaning that when I visited Longman Green,[51] I asked them to introduce me to one of their literary readers. They've written a letter and scheduled an appointment for 3:00 p.m. tomorrow, and I've called and agreed to see him. His name is Zhong! And I don't know why I've written all this. So that the page wouldn't go to waste?

TUESDAY, JANUARY 22, 1962

DEAR JALAL,

I'm writing these few lines in a hurry so that you'll know what's happening. I mailed my letter this morning, meaning my long letter. And this letter is just to keep you informed about my trip, which has at least a 70 percent chance of happening. After mailing the letter I went to see Rafiah at the Jewish Agency for Israel. He gave me your letter to read. Bravo! What a letter. Completely inimitable, in your special style. In short, I told him that your style is entirely unique and that no one could ever imitate you. He was very kind and wrote a letter of invitation and gave it to me. Of course, he hasn't received an answer from their headquarters yet, but he is so optimistic that their answer will come that he prompted me to do all the things I'm writing you about. From there I went straight to Dr. Siassi.[52] I can say in brief that he is one honorable and helpful man. My only option is to get an official passport, and an official passport needs to be approved by the department and the university board. But Dr. Siassi wrote a letter of his own to the university administration so that they can request the passport, and then the plan can proceed. It would be funny if, with all of Dr. Siassi's help, a supporting letter still didn't arrive from the Jewish center. I was about to leave with Dr. Siassi's letter, which was signed and ready within the hour, when I saw that the car had a flat tire, meaning that some kids had let the air out of it. (They were angry that there wasn't vacation yesterday on the first of Bahman.) Not only the air out of my tire, but from all the cars. I died laughing. Finally Dr. Majid Shibani's[53] chauffeur came to help all of us and inflated the tires, and replaced one of the punctured tires, and I got there, I mean I reached the administration building at exactly 11:15 a.m. Dr. Shibani also parked there, and it was decided that he would write his letter and give it to the president of the university, who would sign it tomorrow, and I could go and get my official passport. Now it depends on my luck: Will I see you there? Will I come? Is it possible, for instance, that you could leave on the second or third of February, so that by that time I'll be ready, my issues resolved, and these descendants of the children of Israel will give their permission? How fun it would be to see you in a foreign country! If I come, we'll go to see Al-Aqsa. In any case, Dr. Siassi has never done what he did for me for anyone else, though it was partially out of pity. He said, "You need a vacation, and I'm doing this of my own volition." Anyway, I'll write you as soon as it's a sure thing.

Tonight I'm eating dinner at the home of Hussein Tavakoli,[54] who is also being very kind, and Kameli, too—I shouldn't be sarcastic—I've caused him enough trouble.[55] If I come to Israel, I'm bringing those two letters with me, which by now have turned into three. But according to the tentative plan I made with Rafiah (you sometimes write Rafi'a, sometimes Rafia, and sometimes Rafiah) for the first five days you and I will travel together. I'm bringing enough cigarettes for both of us and enough money for you, at least enough that if you don't want to come back, we'll have enough for a month of living expenses, and cigarettes. But as for my own plan, I'll have two days of participating in an archaeological dig, two lectures at the university in Jerusalem, seeing museums, meeting some writers and poets and one or two women's organizations. Rafiah asked, "Don't you want to meet the foreign minister?" I said, "Who is the foreign minister?" He said, "Golda Meir." I said, "Well, what would I have to say to that world-traveling woman politician?" I was about to say "that old witch." But I said that if I had time it might be nice to see the kibbutz where Ben-Gurion and Golda Meir started out, and also a moshav, which he corrected: moshavim.

When I was coming home I ran into Gohar Morad.[56] On the way we picked up Mehri[57] and the three of us came back home and ate lunch together. And I explained the situation to them. And now I ask you: why have we all become political without having even studied political science in college, and why are the only people who are not political our politicians, who make policy by dictation, from the shah to the prime minister to the representatives in the Majles? They both send heartfelt greetings to you. But has Shams lost his mind, working for free in the Archaeology Institute? Have I gone crazy to allow it? I know Dr. Nigahban[58] from America and I'm mulling over what to do.

YOURS,

SIMIN

2:30 P.M., FRIDAY, JANUARY 25, 1963. LONDON

DEAREST SIMIN,

I've got good news. We are going to see each other in Tel Aviv. Perhaps you know already and have set out, as the Israeli diplomats in London know and have informed me. When I mailed today's letter, I went to our embassy with three boxes of books, and from there I telephoned the Israeli embassy information center. They said I'm going Monday, and that they are going to give me a special passport-like document for entering Israel. They also said, "Your wife will join you in Tel Aviv." A hundred myriad thanks! If only I had asked them to send you to Europe.

In any case, I'm over the moon that I have produced no legitimate heir and that because of Israel I pushed back my return to Tehran. And because in the end you also have the opportunity to escape for a few days from that house of mourning to breathe, and be ready for me to woo you and to brush the dust off your clothes, and to warm you and fatten you up and comfort you—how many others have you comforted?—and what do you say if we never go back? Once we've seen Israel, will we be able to run away through the high passes and return to that ruined part of the world and get back to work? Mrs. Lambton will also be at today's lecture, Farzad told me. They really announced the news with trumpets blaring, and I prepared myself for enlivening the youth and talking sharply, sophisticatedly, and directly, subtly skinning them with implication and innuendo. I've prepared my notes and I'm only home now writing because I came to find airmail letters in order to write to you, my dear, the good news that you're going to Tel Aviv.

I organized a lunch this afternoon for Farzad and Mahmoudi, and Jadali also joined us. The cost of the lunch was two and a half pounds; Jadali contributed one pound. He wanted to split it, but since he doesn't drink, I didn't take more than one. At least its better than nothing. Also Mahmoudi has some little things that he is going to give me to bring back for him, and of course I happily accepted. I think I'll have enough space. Anyway, I now have seventy pounds, twenty of which is for the rest of my stay at the hotel, and I need thirty pounds for the two days in Amsterdam before I get to Tel Aviv and ten pounds for shopping. In any event, bring money with you for Israel just in case. And don't forget the Oshno cigarettes. And also your cigarettes. Changing cigarettes is very harmful for addicts like us. Give the house key to Shams or anyone else you want and come with your mind at ease. And really, think about the possibility of not going back. I'm sorely tempted, and now that I'm sitting here, nothing is missing but your presence sitting across from me listening to me tell you about this long and tiresome journey, and then sharing your troubles with me with your sweet voice and your sweet body and, really, what a pity it is that I don't have you with me right now. Also remember to give the car to Kameli, since it is possible we won't go back and he will be able to sell it, so you don't have to bring it to Tajrish. . . Now you'll probably say that this old fool has gone crazy! But I'm thinking rationally. When I can so easily be the focus of attention here and do my work, and they are courting me, directly and indirectly inviting me to stay, what reason is there to go back? Apart from you? And you're also getting rid of that evil, filthy house of mourning, worthy only of the shah's mother's beard!

In any case, that's enough. I'll leave some space for the evening's report and will mail this letter tomorrow morning. And I know that after this letter I won't be able to write you more than one or two more. You must be going on February 2 and I have to figure out when I need to send my letters so that they reach you by February 1. In other words, at most I can send letters until January 28. Three more days, meaning I will send my last letter next Monday. Or Tuesday. And I'll certainly get two or three letters from you in that time. Waiting for your letters, sending a kiss, and hoping to see you soon. And this is the reward of patience that I get rock candy![59] Let us be blessed. You can see how happy I am!

SATURDAY, JANUARY 26, 1963

DEAR JALAL,

I think this is the last letter I will send, my dearest, assuming it reaches you. I mailed my long letter on Tuesday and haven't written anything since, because there has been so much to do—writing that letter, getting my passport, and the other preparations for the trip. Meaning, I have had one foot in the Jewish Agency, another at the university, and also the prime minister's office, and it is altogether bad timing: today is the referendum and things have been so busy with strikes and meetings. In short, Wednesday was the women's strike that resulted in giving them the vote. I ended up being so involved that I brought the university's list of demands to the prime minister's office. Meaning that in all this disorder I had to take a letter from Dr. Siassi, from the university secretariat and with Dr. Farhad's[128] signature, and then bring it to the prime minister's office and wait for them. I went there this morning, and it was half-closed because of the referendum, but it was clear that my paper had gone to the security services. So tomorrow morning I'm going to grab it. If they give me permission and I get a diplomatic passport, perhaps I can join you on February 1. My heart is racing. I feel just like a lover who has a date with his beloved and worries he can't make the meeting, but I also fear this encounter. When my long letter arrives, will you understand why?

The National Front held a rally yesterday, despite not having permission from the police, but farmers attacked them and injured many. Everyone has been struck with political fever, as you say, but if they all recover, I'll let you know. Now let's speak our own words. I was supposed to have class Wednesday evening, but it was canceled, and Thursday I spent all my time preparing for the trip, and at noon Shams, Islam, and Mohasses came for lunch. Of course, those two are Shams's escorts, and I gave him permission to throw a party for his friends at his brother's house. Anyway, I was busy with Mohasses's speeches about "abstract art" until evening, and then I drove them home and picked up the children. Yesterday I cleaned my clothes for the trip and in the evening went to Victoria's house for Mani's[62] birthday, which was very nice, and we stayed until ten at night, and this morning, after the prime minister's office, I went to Rafiah. It worked. They are taking care of all the expenses for the ticket and the stay (seventeen days). If that passport is ready, you're going to regret it. So, if the passport is ready, they will let you know and I will inevitably write to you myself. But to what address? I don't know. I hope all is well and can't wait to see you in Tel Aviv, my love. In any case, as ordered, I will be bringing eight hundred toman. I won't bother you any more—

YOUR SIMIN

THAT SAME DAY, JANUARY 26

What sort of Jalal are you? In all the years we have been together, you must have noticed that I never smashed anyone's jug, and I've watered the jug of anyone who's asked as far as I was able. The only ones I've ever knocked over were the jugs of bastards, roughnecks who carry on being crude even with dry, broken jugs. At least as I see it,

I have poured water in your jug most of all, and now, from the other side of the world, you're the one who has taken my jug and smashed it. Whenever I hinted and was jealous in earlier letters, so that you might speak and give me the explanation you owe me, you didn't notice and passed everything off as my pain over the loss of my sister, or you thought that, as you said, I was only messing around. Oblivious to the fact that time, as it passes, casts a healing spell, and that this pain from your breaking my jug will also heal in time. I even wrote you that two confusing letters arrived on January 5, but you didn't ask me seriously about the contents of those letters. (The post also suddenly seems unreliable to me, for the post can be a homewrecker). January 5 two letters arrived for me. One in Persian, well written and unsigned, from December 29. The other was in English, written on official paper on December 28 and signed by someone you refer to in your letters. Both were mailed from Amsterdam. Now a third letter has arrived, also in Persian and in that same good handwriting, which was sent from London and confirms the contents of the first letter. Reading these letters was no picnic. Neither is writing this letter, the main part of which I'm copying from my journal. And I imagine that reading it will be no picnic for you. At first I thought I would show the letters to Shams, but what sin did he commit that he has to bear all your burdens on his shoulders, and besides, he would take your side. Afterward I thought of Vicky, who inevitably would take my side. I thought it would be better to bring it to Maleki, and I invited myself over to his house Monday night.

I won't confuse you. The official letter, in English, informed me that it had reached their attention that you and one of the guides, named Hilda. . . had developed a close relationship and that you spent your free time with her. They wrote that they had summoned her and had warned her and reminded her that the result would be breaking up the family of one of the invitees, but she answered that her personal life was her own business. They asked her if this relationship was serious, and she answered, "I don't want to be any man's second wife." They warned me so that afterward I wouldn't be able to blame them. Perhaps I will send these letters to you, and if I go to Israel, I am absolutely bringing them with me. In the first Persian letter, after mentioning the details, it said, "As of now it has been four days since we last heard from Mr. Al-e Ahmad. A certain Miss Hilda came looking for him one morning and put his luggage in a car, and they left. We saw them together one day in the museum and another day in an Amsterdam park." In the second letter they informed me that Hilda is now living at the hotel where Mr. Al-e Ahmad booked a room for her—a suite. You yourself wrote that on the way to Tel Aviv you will go to Amsterdam to see the Brunai and that you have high hopes for Holland. Is it impossible to fly directly from London to Tel Aviv?

One side of my head hurts. I remember Farouzanfar,[62] who used to point to one side of his head in class and say the same, and I once asked my father about the professor's headache. He told me it was migraines. He recommended lavender incense and smoking lavender instead of cigarettes. I'm going to go get some of that lavender incense.

I've already told you that I'm going to mail this letter, but I'm still debating whether to mail it, and if I don't, then you will consider my long letter from January 13 as a replacement for this one.[63]

Anyway, I went to Maleki's house. Sabihe was there, too. I told them what happened and gave the letters to Maleki. He said, "My eyes are no good, and I don't know English anyway. You translate and read it, so that Sabihe can hear as well." Sabihe became angrier than I have ever seen her. I almost screamed, and in the midst of crying and screaming I remembered the night when you first brought me to Maleki's house so that you could introduce me to them as your wife-to-be, and, with the excuse of preparing the salad, she pulled me into the kitchen and explained that being a politician's wife is no easy thing. "I have experience," she said. "From time to time, with a bent neck, a package of fruit, and a lunch pot, you have to go from this prison to that prison and speak to people with a queasy stomach. . . and Jalal is sickly also. . ." Sabihe was yelling now. She told me, "On that night you said, 'I am no thin, fragile reed. I retain the right to divorce.' Good, Simin. Go and get divorced and send the document along with those letters to Jalal." Maleki smiled and said, "So Jalal has split with you as well." Then he said, "Jalal wrote *Gharbzadegi*, but he has found refuge in the West, with a Western woman." Maleki started crying, too. I kissed his bald head and put my arm over Sabihe's shoulder and kissed her as well. Both of them were taken aback by my calm. I said, "This morning I did an hour of yoga and took a Valium." I said to Sabihe, "Writing the first chapter of my shared life with Jalal meant deciding that love was more important than reason, but writing the second chapter of that book and finishing it is more difficult. It's true that I can divorce him, but reason's victory over love takes time. I must write the end of this book with care, considering all the angles." Maleki put his hand on Sabihe's back and said, "Simin is right. Now is not the time for feminist slogans," and tried to send her to the kitchen to calm down. Sabihe said, "Khalil, don't play at being in charge. At least let this woman teach men a lesson."

Maleki said, "Most of the content of these Persian letters is prejudice, jealousy about Jalal's artistic abilities, and revenge, but it nevertheless confirms the official letter.

Therefore we have to believe that this situation is real." I asked, "What was the point of that official letter? It's not like I went to the court of arbitration at The Hague and complained about this guide." Maleki had no information about the laws of Holland and also confessed that he pays little attention to his comrades' family problems and asked that I answer his questions, saying, "Your opinion is important to me, Simin." I told him directly, "At the beginning of our marriage I considered you my rival, but now, having recognized your moral uniqueness and steadfast personality, you know that I've trusted you and shared my problems with you." He asked, "Has Jalal been writing less and are his letters unkind?" I said, "On the contrary, he writes a lot. His last letter was even more affectionate than those at the beginning of the trip, perhaps because he feels guilty."

He said, "You have had a unique life together, the kind often found in the West, but here your relationship is uncommon and has inspired jealousy. Wasn't this kind of relationship the reason for your honest love for each other?" I answered, "For my part, absolutely; for Jalal's, I'm not 100 percent sure. Otherwise, he wouldn't have gone back on it in these last four months. I have made our house a sanctuary for him. Why does Jalal suddenly not want me, after having made his life safe and secure? His morning yogurt and honey are always ready, his cigarettes and sundries are ready, he is provided with the perfect reception for his groupies, his juice is at hand, and his property increased—with little financial help from Jalal. Perhaps you want to say that Jalal has kept me for my competence in such worldly affairs. Most of his friends share the same opinion. They have even made references to Khadijah and the Prophet Muhammad,[64] but Jalal always answered, 'Simin is my Ai-sha.'[65] Of course, Jalal had obligations to his mother and sometimes helped one or two of his sisters financially."

Maleki asked, "Did you pressure him because of that?" I said, "Is it possible for anyone to pressure him? You want to say that now Jalal is seeking a release for this pressure? No pressure was involved at all. On the contrary, I gave him a lot of freedom, and, as for our financial relations, there was never any 'this is mine' and 'this is yours.'" He said, "You know that Jalal was known among the comrades as 'the Fretful Sayyid.'" And I said that Eprim Eshaq[66] called me "the sheikh's wife." He said, "If Jalal still loves you, after this, that love will be rote and clerical." I said, "If that's the case, I'm not interested."

He asked, "When he became angry, did you respond in kind?" I said, "When he was really boiling over, sometimes I let loose my serpent tongue, as he called it. A person can only endure so much before it comes out in the end. But most of the time I left him to himself, knowing that two hours later he would feel sorry and say such loving words and express so much love that my heart would melt."

He said, "Now let's turn to this. You're at a crossroads, what should you do? In my opinion you should continue your letters as usual. But sometimes drop hints and be jealous. As for now, don't get a divorce. I've arranged your trip to Israel through Ezri. Take the letters to Israel with you and solve the problem like the two civilized people that you are. Jalal is a worthy person. He is also an idealist. . ." Then the children came and we ate lunch, the stew that only Sahibe knows how to make, but we three ate very little and I basically had only salad. Peroz noticed our silence and asked me, "Auntie Simin, has something happened?"

And now you and I are face to face. Is this situation serious? You, who always bravely trusted in clarity, and I, who never did (that it is really clear), why weren't you brave enough to write me the truth yourself? I said to you, if you have to do something, do it, as long as you let me know. Because I feel cursed in this crisis. But you turned to Hilda so blatantly that even her bosses noticed. Why did you leave me? Oh, Mr. Arabic, *lamadha taraktani*? You know that I'm not Job. Just as you're not my creator. Why did you erase the laughter from my lips? When I was in America, I innocently went to a party and even wrote you about it, and you became possessive and I was forced to choose solitude. Once I walked with an aged, frail professor to mail you a letter. You became so suspicious of me that I didn't even turn in my exam for that professor's class. In one of your letters from that trip you anxiously warned me that my love for my nieces and nephews shouldn't be more than my love for you. And now you? You yourself? Has the northern chill, or the virtue of ten years of living with me, or a few months in Europe, made you so *développé* that you could do this? Or perhaps you've turned to this woman in order to test your virility once and for all. The first time this woman appeared in your letters was when you said, "a very nice forty-five-year-old woman is our guide." Jalal, you are not going to have children. Certainly not with a forty-five-year-old woman, nice as she may be. Dr. Todd in America told me over and over again that I am as healthy as a horse. Dr. Alfredo (or whatever his name was) in Vienna said it to you himself, and you called me from that doctor's office and told me the news and asked me if I still wanted you. And I made a vow to you in the Spanish Riding School in Vienna, and we sat together for hours and looked at the noble horses dancing to the music, and Prince Aly Khan's[67] horse won the prize. If only one of those horses was here now and I could ride it, four shoes flying and the wind whipping my hair, so that I wouldn't have to write this letter.

I remember during our engagement when I asked you, "Why are you estranged from your father and older brother?" You told me, "My father took a second wife." One day he bought a bag of apples and brought it home, and your mother, who was rocking one of the grandchildren in the cradle, stood up to take the bag of fruit from your father. Your father said, "It is Hajieh's," and pushed the cradle so hard that its handles hit your mother in the chest. And you said that your older brother had you take his second Arab wife back to her father and mother after their divorce—I don't remember if this was in Najaf or Karbala. And they, too, didn't restrain themselves from beating this extra mouth to feed who had returned home, and you paid her father the dower and escaped. I said, "Perhaps one reason why you turned to the Tudeh Party was these experiences." You said, "It's not impossible." Perhaps my compassion and pity for Iranian women comes from seeing the injustice suffered by the women of your family. By your two sisters and Tayybeh,[68] which I witnessed myself. Your older sister, when her husband married the daughter of that butcher, took opium twice. Now my heart goes out to that butcher's daughter. Left to her fate, now a servant to your sister, as we saw when we went to Qom. And that mademoiselle who was my favorite sister-in-law, she was the color of ivory. I was about to go traveling, and we were both in our house on Iranshahr Street. In the morning you brought your sister to Dr. Vasuqi, and he examined her chest and announced that he didn't think her tumors were malignant. I still can't stop thinking, why didn't Dr. Vasuqi, who was and is so proficient, check your sister's waist and chest? You brought your sister to our house and told me to make her better. You called me a "heart restorer." Do you remember? I felt the tumors on her chest and your sister said, "I have them below my waist, too." I put my hand there. There were scattered tumors the size of lentils. I asked your sister, "When did you notice them?" She said, "It's that jerk," or something even worse. She meant her husband. Who saw a girl riding her bicycle in Mashhad, picked her up, and brought her home. One day your sister was doing her ablutions by the pool, when the girl saw her and told that bastard, "But you have such a pretty wife," and dropped everything and left. Your sister said, "Then he took me to Mashhad." I asked, "Because of the girl?" She said no, seemingly because the jerk wanted to apologize. Then Marzieh came for a visit with Mehdi and Hassan. . . enough. One of the children got lost, and your sister said that because of the worry and excitement about a lost child she struck her chest and noticed the tumors.

Do you know why you saw Golestan[69] in a dream? Because you have done exactly what Golestan did. But know that I am not Fakhri, not your mother, not your sisters, and not Tayybeh. I am leaving you. Perhaps I am a small person, but I am not so slight that I will give up my body to scorn. How much have I saved to get to where I am? How many thousands of pages of books have I read? How many thousands of pages of journals have I written? How many hundreds of hours of classes have I taught? And my accomplishments and pride are certainly not inferior to yours. I claim that I am advancing Iranian women and fighting for their rights. Anyone who speaks has to act first. I can and must be a model for Iranian women. But even if I'm not, then this is the model I will offer to Iranian women. I will show them that this life that was forced on us is a mistake. Accommodating tyranny, abuse, these attachments are all compounded mistakes. Perhaps I have evaded your slaps. But I am coming out of this beating clean and ready, and crossing over this border I will be a new person, a new woman, and I will make Iranian women realize that they have to be new women. I am not some old brick in a condemned building that can fall and shatter without consequence. I thought, we have so few opportunities in this world; what's better than warming ourselves with the heat of love before we go? Now in the chill of disloyalty I'm warming myself with the reservoir of my mind. I am like those tropical plants that produce thick leaves so that they have a reserve of water. I have this reserve, and I will extend it to Iranian women. But I'm not your enemy, and if you'd like, we can still be friends— the welcome friendship of a man and woman when both have transcended sexuality. You know, I'm thankful for the sweet nights and days we had together. Thank you for the times when you told me (and once when you wrote me from Yazd), "Simin, you are my guiding light, the magnet that attracts all my being." Thank you for the day when two doves, a male and a female, strutted and courted in our yard, and you said, "The fatter one is you and the skinny one is me"—and for other such kind words, phrases, and sentences. Thank you for curing me of my laziness, for making my life with you exciting. This was my share of love. That's how it was from the very beginning. I am so thankful.

6:00 A.M., JANUARY 27

I've taken a cholera vaccine and my temperature is 101.3. This morning I'm mailing this letter. Whatever you have to do, do it. If this letter reaches you in London, or if you get it in Amsterdam. (Since you might not be in London, I'm sending the letter to Amsterdam. To the address and name of that person who wrote the official letter; this is also, in a way, an answer for him.) In any case, whether in London, Amsterdam, or wherever, go to the Iranian embassy and give power of attorney to Shams to take care of your business in Tehran. I took Shams's details from his file in the Archaeology Institute: Shams al-Din Sadat Al-e Ahmad, the child of Haj Sayyid Ahmad Taleqani, ID 392000. (We don't have an embassy in Israel and recognize Israel de facto. Ezri told me this, according to Maleki, to stress how difficult it was for me to go to Israel.) Afterward, when you go to Amsterdam, marry Hilda. I have enough money with me. I sold the *brilliant* broach that Mr. Hashmat al-Mulk[70] gave me on the night of our engagement and a decorated cup and plate through "*Beman*." From Israel, go back to your wife and, through Peter Avery[71] or others, or even Jamalzadeh,[71] you'll be able to find work and stay in Europe. That's all up to you now. I prefer to stay silent than play at being a commanding patriarch. But I might stay for those five days we had planned to tour Israel together, or I might not come at all. Getting the divorce would take me half an hour, without even needing to mention your sterility. In any case, with Shams's help, I am selling the house and most of the furniture and other things, which have no meaning anymore, and Shams will send you your portion in dollars. I don't want a dower either. When there is no affection, you can forget the dower.

But I'm leaving this opening for love: if it becomes clear to me that your relationship with Hilda was based only on lust and that you never intended to humiliate me or be disloyal (from reading your journals, and your reasoning and behavior; if we get back together, you can read my journals as well), I'll consider those letters unread and, with the fever I have, will treat them all as a nightmarish delirium. But on the condition that we don't let this hang over us and make each other's lives bitter, that you don't resurrect the past, and that there be no further exchanges of letters or gifts. Because clinging to the past cheapens a person. As far as I can tell, your relationship has been going on for almost a month now, and if she's pregnant, it's already showing. Tell Hilda she has won. I remember Miriam,[73] my friend in America. The last day of class, I got sixteen votes and she got fifteen. She kissed me and said, "You won." But now she is one of the best writers in Texas and has published many stories, with a collection of stories forthcoming. And another classmate who got eight votes (Hannah)[74] is now a first-class writer in New York and they're adapting one of her novels for a film, and my life has become a film in this shallow pit of the world (in Hedayat's[75] words). I am not wounded by you. Don't be pained by me. We are not the first husband and wife to separate, and we won't be the last.

SIMIN DANESHVAR

9 A.M., MONDAY, JANUARY 28, 1963. STILL LONDON

DEAREST SIMIN,

Thankfully a letter arrived from you today—the airmail letter from Tuesday, January 22 in which you mentioned

another long letter that hasn't yet arrived, and perhaps still
will. First of all, thank you for writing your name and address on the back of the envelope. Secondly, things have
worked out very well, because it also occurred to me that
I would get to Tel Aviv one or two days later, the details of
which I've written you. It's up to me. I can spend a day in
Amsterdam or Paris or both. The truth is that I didn't want
to stay here in London, where everyone thinks I've become
so enamored of them—though, in truth, I have. I wanted,
for instance, to give them the cold shoulder and say, "Yes,
thank you for your kindness, but I have to go. . ." If I knew
what day you would be there then it would be possible
to go to Tel Aviv even later, but I don't have the patience
anymore. Get moving and endure a little longer, and, in
exchange, I'm going to kiss you from head to toe. I know
how you end up chasing your own tail when you're alone.
Then, of course, we're going to visit Al-Aqsa. You've lec-
tured so much on the Dome of the Rock, you have to see it
from up close. Also, Siassi hasn't done anything for you
out of pity; he just wanted to shut you up. No one knows
how much you and I are suffering from being apart.
Others run from their husbands and wives, just like you
nearly did that time in America. But you know that I never slipped away from you—or from the country. On the
contrary, I didn't want to leave behind such a prize, and
then we said and wrote that I came here searching for a

safe refuge, and now I've found it. Either Paris or London. Whichever you prefer. One stroke of the pen to Avery or Lambton (whom I'm scheduled to meet on Wednesday evening as I wrote you, and I've brought that *Fashandak* book as a final exploit) is enough, and they'll gracefully accept us. Everything depends on you. Really, I think it's possible that when our time ends in Israel and Tel Aviv, we won't return home. What do you say? We'll talk about all of this in detail. And in any case, thank God my arrow reached the mark and I got you moving. And Rafiah in his letter accepted my suggestion of writing a book but didn't mention anything about a contract, so I will have to make him understand that without funding it's just unleavened bread.[76] And he knows about that better than we do.

Anyway, now that I have to get on the road, the weather in London has gotten better. For the past three days. The ice and snow have melted and the water is flowing in the pipes. Did I write or not that for twenty days we had only boiling water in the pipes and they left the cold-water tank empty for fear that it would burst again? And, according to the radio, during this time there were sixteen-thousand incidents of pipes and tanks bursting in London, just like in our own country, and the snow didn't pile up much before the weather got warmer and it melted, and now, aside from Hyde Park, which is covered in hideous, black snow, there's no snow anywhere. All the roofs are clean. I'm on the fourth floor and reign over the roofs of London. For three days I've woken up in the morning to the chirping of sparrows. When will we two sparrows once more wake up to each other's chirping?

Okay, that's enough. I will leave the last few lines at the bottom of the page blank to tell you what happens in the Israeli embassy, where I have to go to get my entrance visa. Goodbye for now, my love, and in hopes to see you soon in the Promised Land, my Shirazi Zuleikha! Though I'd rather eat shit than be Joseph.[77]

10:30 A.M., THE SAME DAY, ON THE LONDON UNDERGROUND

DEAREST SIMIN,

I just left the Israeli embassy, with my visa on a separate piece of paper, that says that there is one person accompanying me: my spouse. And now I'm going (after a change) to Oxford Circus where I have to go to the publications department of the British Council; I'm asking them to send me ten or twenty important London periodicals. In fact, I went to go buy them. But the price of one issue of each periodical was about five pounds, and we can ask them to send them to us (the train is shaking terribly) for free, and we will translate them or publicize them in the Persian press in exchange. That's all. Your love.

11:00 A.M., WEDNESDAY, JANUARY 30, 1963. LONDON

DEAREST SIMIN,

This is the last letter I am sending from London. And I don't know if it will reach you or not. In any case, have a good flight, unless you've already departed, and I'll see you soon. Yesterday I received your letter from January 25.[78] Just like my own letter, it was very short and only contained information about your itinerary. I'm leaving tomorrow morning. Two days on the road—on purpose, to give time for you to arrive and for the Jews to prepare— and then I land Monday at 8:00 p.m. Tel Aviv time. Without jinxing it or inshallah. I saw Mrs. Lambton yesterday over lunch and we had the usual conversation. I'm going to visit her again this evening at the School of Oriental Studies in London, with Haydari. Last night I went to a cocktail party organized by PEN and met several people who are planning to come to Tehran in April. It was the first time that during one party, three unknown women, as soon as we were introduced, asked me about the weather in Tehran in April and what clothes they should bring with them, and I was shocked at how strange things have become. These people are coming to participate in a literary conference, but their minds are preoccupied with clothes and fashion. Anyway. Perhaps even if they invite us to this whatever-it-is, we won't go, because perhaps the shah is presenting it, and I have no patience for all that nonsense. But, in any case, we must host these people in Tehran some time. Your obligations are gradually increasing. First the Dutch, and now these others, too. In exchange, I've scrutinized their work a bit. Also, I'm going to change this worn-out shoulder bag and buy a new one. And yesterday I bought you a book on the history of art for five pounds—they ship it themselves for that price—and perhaps they will send it today, or perhaps they sent it yesterday. I'm happy I managed to fulfill your request. Also, you'll see your loving Jalal in less than a week in Tel Aviv. If something is left from the Shiraz money, bring it with you, along with the cigarettes.

Jadali just brought your strange letter. I'm calling you and waking you up. Wake up! To hell with the plans.

NOTES

INTRODUCTION

1   Khamenei's recollections are quoted on pages 39-40 of Shams Al-e Ahmad's introduction to *Safar be Velayat-e 'Izra'il* (Tehran: Revaq, 1984).

2   The best English translation of *Gharbzadegi* is R. Campbell's rendition as *Occidentosis: A Plague from the West*, with an introduction by Hamid Algar (Berkeley: Mizan Press, 1984). The quote can be found on page 28 of that edition.

3   This statement appears in a letter from Simin Daneshvar to Al-e Ahmad from January 22, 1963, published in *Nameh-ha-ye Simin Daneshvar va Jalal Al-e Ahmad*, edited by Masoud Jafari (Tehran: Nilufar, 2005), 3: 342-343.

4   *Dar Khedmat va Khianat-e Roshanfikran* (Tehran: Khwarezmi, 1978), 336-337.

5   I am quoting from page seventy-one of Yaron Ezrahi's *Rubber Bullets: Power and Conscience in Modern Israel* (New York: Farrar, Straus, and Giroux, 1996). This section also owes a great deal to Bernard Avishai's *The Tragedy of Zionism: How its Revolutionary Past Haunts Israeli Democracy* (New York: Helios Pres, 2002).

THE ISRAELI REPUBLIC

1   In Islamic exegetical literature, St. George is a prophet of the Children of Israel who lived after Jesus. Al-e Ahmad is referring here to a common Persian proverb. A rooster, having been caught by a fox, makes a last request that the fox say the name of one of the prophets, "so that, because of its sanctity, it will be easier for me to give up my life." While the rooster's plan is to flee when the fox opens its mouth to speak, the fox itself is more cunning: saying *Jirjis*—"St. George" in Persian—the fox's mouth only clenches tighter. Dying it says, "Damn you, that from all the prophets you chose St. George!". [Translator's note]

2   In Islamic tradition, as in the Bible (Exodus 2:12), Moses' murder of the Egyptian is a turning point that begins his prophetic career. However, in the Qur'an, Moses is not rebuked for the murder but forgiven by God (Surat al-Qasas 28:16). [Translator's note]

3   The tombs of Daniel, Esther, and Mordechai are all important shrines in Iran. [Translator's note]

4   This is borrowed from a biblical statement (Isaiah 56:5) that Yahweh promises to preserve his name and hand (memorial) for the people who keep such and such religious rituals.

5   Approximately 600–900 kilograms, almost a ton. [Translator's note]

6   Al-e Ahmad refers to the memorial *Martiri delle Fosse Ardeatine* in Rome, with a bronze door made by the contemporary sculptor Mirco. [Translator's note]

7   Nader Naderpour was a modernist poet, member of Maleki's Third Force and friend of Al-e Ahmad. [Translator's note]

8   In the monthly magazine *Andisheh-ye No* (New Thinking) that Anvar Khame'i produced, in 1948. It did not last more than three issues.

9   *Science and Life (Elm va Zendegi)* was an magazine edited by Khalil Maleki, an Iranian intellectual, socialist, and one of Al-e Ahmad's mentors. The magazine was first published in 1950 and included contributions by some of the most prominent Iranian leftist writers. Al-e Ahmad published many of his articles there. [Translator's note]

10 Two of us translated this book at the same time; Dr. Vasuqi and Ali Asghar Khebrehzadeh's translation was even published at exactly the same time that I myself translated André Gide's *Return from the USSR*.

11 Once in the magazine *Mehrgan*, and afterward in the preface to the second edition of *The Unwanted Woman*.

12 Regarding the relations between Egypt and Iran: Princess Fawzia's departure, and the bad behavior of guests in Fawzia's wedding [Fawzia was the first wife of Mohammad Reza Shah Pahlavi, and sister of Egypt's King Faruk; she and Mohammad Reza Shah married in 1939 and divorced in 1948] (lack of water in the bathroom, broken silverware, etc.); the beheading of Abu Taleb Yazdi [an Iranian youth who was sentenced to execution in 1904 for vomiting while participating in the Hajj in Mecca]; the independence of India and Pakistan—and the films and such produced on this issue; the political questions of Shahrivar and pro-Russian influence [Allied forces invaded Iran on August 22, 1941 and removed Reza Shah from power on September 16th of that year. In the Iranian calendar both those dates fall within the month of Shahrivar,

1320]; who determined to attack the entire Middle East from that side; changing the center of the waterway to Russia which before went via Turkey and Egypt to Europe. And now it is via Russia and America—the expansion of radio and television and the facility of getting news from all over the world . . . and the succession of the English in the struggle with spirituality in place of France and the West—and finally the cutting off of relations with Iraq and Egypt after the 1953 coup d'état. These are the reasons for our remaining cut off from Egypt and the Arab world. [Translator's notes in brackets]

13 This "period of ignorance" is the time in Arabian history prior to Muhammad's revelation. [Translator's note]

14 The Barmakids were a powerful Iranian family of state secretaries and advisers during the early Abbasid period (c. 730–803) who originated from the reigon of Balkh in today's Afghanistan. Early Muslim historians believed the family to be descended from a line of Zoroastrian priests. [Translator's note]

15 Abu Abdallah al-Hosayn b. Muhammad Amid and his son Abul Fadl Mohammad b. Amid both served as courtiers and important writers in Arabic in courts in northern Persia and Transoxania in the tenth century. Abu Abdallah was born to a family of lowly Persian background in Qom (now a major Shia center). [Translator's note]

16 Descendants and clients of the seventh century general Al-Mohallab b. Abi Sufrah, the Banu Mohallab were an influential family of prominent courtiers, Arabic poets, and men of culture in the first centuries of Islam. Al-Mohallab's father was reported to have been a Persian weaver. [Translator's note]

17 A Barmakid vizier who ordered the stamping of gold coins. [Translator's note]

18 A clay brick made out of soil from shrines in Najaf or Karbala, Iraq on which Shiite worshipers rest their foreheads during prayer. [Translator's note]

19 One of the companions of the Prophet Muhammad who conquered Egypt and the Levant. [Translator's note]

20 Prominent Italian actress of the 1960s who stared in, among other films, *Solomon and Sheba* (1959). [Translator's note]

21 During the 1951 Abadan crisis, Iranian Prime Minister Muhammad Mossadegh nationalized Iran's oil, wresting control from the UK-controlled Anglo-Persian Petroleum Company. This seizure led directly to the 1953 CIA and MI6 backed coup that overthrew Mossadegh and restored the shah to power. [Translator's note]

22 As it is written in the Holy Qur'an: "The Arabs of the desert are the worst in unbelief and hypocrisy . . ." (9:97).

23   Two small mountains located inside the holy precinct in Mecca. During the Hajj, pilgrims travel seven times back and forth between the two locations in commemoration of Hagar's seven trips while searching for water for Ishmael. [Translator's note]

24   In Iranian culture, Arabs are often derided as "lizard eaters," uncivilized dwellers of the desert, as opposed to the city-dwelling and urbane Iranians. The classical source for this association is Nasir Khusraw's travelogue, the *Safarnameh*, which served as a model for Al-e Ahmad's own prose style and travel writing. The *Safarnameh* is an account of the eleventh-century Iranian writer's travels from Eastern Iran through the Levant to Egypt and Mecca. Khusraw writes of travels with local tribes in the deserts of the Arabian Peninsula: "Whenever my companions saw a lizard they killed and ate it. The Arabs, wherever they are, milk their camels for drink. I could neither eat lizards nor drink camels' milk; therefore, wherever I saw a kind of bush that yielded small berries the size of lentils, I picked a few and subsisted on that." From Nasir Khusraw, *Book of Travels*, translated by Wheeler M. Thackston, Jr. (Costa Mesa, CA: Mazda, 2001), 108. [Translator's note]

25   The story of the Seven Sleepers of Ephesus is an originally Christian tale of a group of youths who, fleeing Roman persecution, hid inside a cave, fell asleep, and miraculously awoke hundreds of years later. A version of this story appears also in the Qur'an (18:7–26) and is expounded upon by classical Muslim exegetes. [Translator's note]

26   *Urshelim* [Jerusalem]: *ur* (city) + *shelim* (peace) = the city of peace.

27   The same that in Islamic and Arabic terminology became *jahanam* [Hell].

28   They call their national assembly by this name.

29   The widest part of Israel, in the Negev desert, is 110 kilometers across, and the most narrow strip of land, between the Mediterranean Sea and the heights of Samaria (which is in Jordanian hands), is only 15 kilometers wide.

30   The statistics for 1962 say that the population of Israel is composed of the following:

The total population: 2,232,300 persons. And here is also the ratio of increase in the Jewish percentage of that same statistic:

The number of Jews: 1,984,000 persons. In 1918, there were a total of 56,671 Jews in Palestine.

The number of Muslims: 172,000 persons. In 1931, there were a total of 174,000 Muslims in Palestine.

The number of Christians: 52,000 persons. In 1940, there were a total of 468,635 Christians in Palestine.

The number of Druze (a Shiite sect): 24,000 persons. In 1948 there were a total of 1,762,741 Druze in Palestine.

31 *Sabra* (cactus) is, in fact, a kind of wild fig, with many sharp thorns. Its fruit is sweet and it can grow to double the height of a person, and it is tolerant of a lack of water. In that country they use this plant for hedges.

32 Quoted from Israel, *Demographic Yearbook*, No. 14, and United Nations, *Demographic Yearbook*, 1963:

Of the general population, the number of Arab students in Israel is 21.1 percent. In Egypt, 11.6 percent; in Lebanon, 17.8 percent; in Jordan, 17.6 percent.

But of the total number of school attendees, the number of students in high school is only 5 percent, whereas in Egypt that same number is 12.5 percent; in Lebanon, 14.8 percent; in Jordan, 21.4 percent.

The number of students in vocational schools out of the total number of school attendees is 0.4 percent; while in Egypt, it is 3.5 percent; in Lebanon, 0.4 percent; in Jordan, 0.6 percent.

Of the total population of school attendees, the number of students in higher education schools in Israel is 0.4 percent; in Egypt, 4.4 percent; in Lebanon, 1.7 percent; and there are no statistics available for Jordan.

These figures are quoted from page 237 of Simha Flapan's article "Les arabes en Israel," published in a special September, 1966 issue of the French magazine *Esprit*, titled "Des Israeliens parlent d'Israel."

33 These are the names of two mutually hostile urban factions that divided most Iranian cities from the late fifteenth century until the early twentieth century. The two factions often fought public battles, usually at the time of festivals and sometimes at the instigation of local rulers; European travelers often make the comparison with the Guelphs and Ghibellines of Florence. Interestingly, Jews and other minorities were not included in this scheme, which was strictly limited to Muslims. For instance, in Isfahan, of the city's twelve wards five were allocated to the Haydari and five to the Ne'mati while the other two were Jewish and Armenian. By 1941, though, with the removal of Reza Shah, the terms Haydari and Ne'mati were used to describe meaningless and archaic squabbles. [Translator's note]

34 From here on, until the point I will indicate, I have freely translated from Jacques Madaule's *Les Juifs et le monde actuel* (Paris: Flamarion, 1963), 91–93.

35 Even today in the Caucasus, a small but diverse group of non-Turkic languages exists.

These are the Tat languages. In other words, they speak in a Persian dialect. And this is interesting that most of them are also Jewish. I saw one of them in Moscow. A tall lady, black haired, "Tajik" and Persian speaking.

36   Text in brackets represents Al-e Ahmad's additions. [Translator's note]

37   Could these not be the remnants of the Albigensians, originally Manichaeans or Mithraists living in that region who at the beginning of the fifteenth century, under the pressure of the Christian Inquisition and from fear, declared themselves to be Jews? (The Albigensians, better known as the Cathars, were a dualistic Christian group opposed to the Catholic Church. In southern France they flourished in particular between the twelfth and the fourteenth centuries. Al-e Ahmad's fifteenth-century date seems to be mistaken. [Translator's note])

38   Ruler of Egypt, 868–884. Son of a Turkish slave. [Translator's note]

39   The famous sixteenth-century traveler and author of *Rihla*, *My Travels*. [Translator's note]

40   Tunisian historian (1332–1406), author of the *Muqaddimah*. [Translator's note]

41   This is the end of what has been copied and translated from pages 91 to 93 of *Les Juifs et le monde actuel*.

42   Hasidim (or Chasidim in the the Yiddish dialect of Poland) are counted as Jewish mystics, who from that time until now have a special area in Jerusalem with their own special customs.

43   This portion of the book first appeared in 1967 in the tenth issue of *Donya-ye Jadid* [new world]. A weekly magazine which, because of the four-page literary miscellany in the middle about art news, the breathing space of Sirus Tahbaz, had a good reputation. And it is no secret that with that same issue it went on a permanent, unfortunate hiatus. In that year, and in that place, this article was anonymous. But one year later, that article was published in Qom in the form of a letter under the name of "Israel, Agent of Imperialism." Its true name, as it appears in Jalal's manuscripts, is as above. [Note by Shams Al-e Ahmad]

44   The last lines of "My Heart of Steel," by Nima Yushij (1896–1960), one of Iran's most important modern poets. Al-e Ahmad was good friends with Yushij and wrote a number of critical studies on his work. The translation of the above lines is adapted from Mahmud Kianush, *Five Poems from Modern Persian Poetry* (Ware, Herts: Rockingham Press, 1996). [Translator's note]

45   The Federation of the Democratic and Socialist Left (Fédération de la gauche

démocrate et socialiste or FGDS) was a conglomerate of French left-wing non-Communist forces. It was founded to support François Mitterrand's candidacy in the 1965 presidential election and to counterbalance the Communist preponderance within the French left. [Translator's note]

46   French politician Pierre Mendès France (1907–1982) was a member of the French National Assembly in 1967. [Translator's note]

47   Daniel Mayer (1909–1996) was a prominent French revolutionary socialist. [Translator's note]

48   Rothschild (1916–2009) and Theodore Klein (b. 1920) raised $10 million for Israel during the 1967 war. Klein was then head of the Committee for Coordination of Solidarity with Israel, which organized the June 6, 1967 meeting at which the donation was announced. The text seems to refer to this donation and this group. [Translator's note]

49   The Hagana was a Jewish paramilitary organization in British Mandatory Palestine, which went on to form the core of the Israel Defenses Forces. [Translator's note]

50   Today's West Bank. [Translator's note]

51   The Iranian equivalent of the Red Cross prior to the 1979 revolution. [Translator's note]

52   From 1956–1962, Georges Pompidou, French prime minister under de Gaulle from 1962 to 1968, served as general manager of Rothschild Fréres Bank. [Translator's note]

53   (1905–1975) French socialist politician and prime minister 1956-1957, during the Suez crisis. [Translator's note]

54   *White and Black Magazine (Majalleh-ye Sepid-o Siyah)* was a popular weekly magazine, comparable to the American *Time*. [Translator's note]

55   An island in the Persian Gulf and a major oil terminal. [Translator's note]

56   The USS *Liberty* was a US Navy technical research ship that was attacked by the Israeli air force and navy on June 8, 1967 just off the coast of Egypt near the town of El-Arish. The attack killed 34 crew members and wounded 171 others. Israeli and American inquiries both determined that the attack had been an accident. However, some have maintained that the ship was attacked deliberately, in order to prevent the Americans from monitoring and broadcasting Israeli troop movements just before Israel's offensive against Syria on June 9. Al-e Ahmad seems to be alluding to a theory of this kind. [Translator's note]

57   Houari Boumediene was the nom de guerre of Mohamad Ben Brahim Boukharouba (1932–1978). Boumediene was a member of the Algerian National Liberation Front

(FLN) and chairman of the Revolutionary Council that overthrew President Ahmed Ben Bella in a 1965 coup. Boumediene ruled Algeria until his death in 1978. [Translator's note]

58   Alexei Nikolayevich Kosygin (1904–1980) was Soviet premier from 1964–1980. Though his position was overshadowed by Brezhnev by the mid-1970s, Kosygin played a leading role in Soviet foreign policy during and after the Six-Day War. [Translator's note]

59   Josip Broz Tito (1892–1980), communist leader of Yugoslavia and major figure in the Non-Aligned Movement. [Translator's note]

60   (1902–1970) A member of the French Section of the Workers' International (SFIO) and a member of the immediate post-war governments as finance minister. [Translator's note]

61   Jean-Jacques Servan-Schreiber (1924–2006) cofounded the weekly *L'Express* in 1953 with Françoise Giroud. The newspaper was associated with radical politics and counted a number of prominent intellectuals in the 1950s and '60s among its contributors, including Camus, Sartre, Malraux, and others. [Translator's note]

62   Pierre Lazareff (1907–1972), the son of Jewish immigrants from Russia, was one of the most important postwar French publishers. [Translator's note]

63   Arthur Goldberg (1908–1990) was a labor lawyer, secretary of labor (1961–1962), Supreme Court justice (1963–1965), and ambassador to the United Nations (1965–1968). [Translator's note]

64   The reference is to a Persian proverb. "Chicken's milk and human life" means every edible thing one can imagine. [Translator's note]

SELECTED CORRESPONDENCE BETWEEN JALAL AL-E AHMAD AND SIMIN DANESHVAR, 1962–1963

1   The meaning of this sentence is not entirely clear. [Translator's note]

2   Zvi Rafiah, an Israeli diplomat in Tehran. [Translator's note]

3   Mohammad Derakhshesh (1917–2005): teacher, member of parliament, and political activist opposed to the shah; minister of education from 1961 until 1962; imprisoned beginning in 1963. [Translator's note]

4   Wife of Ali Jadali Araghi, a Tehran teacher who also received a UNESCO fellowship and travelled throughout Europe with Al-e Ahmad. [Translator's note]

5   Parviz Dariush (1922–2000), a translator and close friend of Al-e Ahmad. [Translator's note]

6   In the September 26, 1962 edition of the German weekly magazine *Der Spiegel*, journalist Gunter Sachs published an exposé on the romantic intrigues of Soraya Esfandiary-Bakhtiari, the ex-wife of Mohammad Reza Pahlavi, shah of Iran. [Translator's note]

7   In a letter from December 7, Daneshvar writes that Shams had a meeting with Derakhshesh. [Translator's note]

8   Farough Farrokhzad, a famous poet. In the letter from December 7, Daneshvar mentions her discussion with Dariush about his "fiery love" for Farrokhzad. [Translator's note]

9   In the letter from December 7, Danshevar writes that Dariush said that she had a bourgeois upbringing and bourgeois ideas. [Translator's note]

10 In the letter from December 7, Daneshvar writes that Jadali's wife sends three letters a week but that Jadali himself complains that she sends no letters. [Translator's note]

11 In the letter from December 7, Daneshvar writes that members of the Tudeh Party had a meeting to discuss *Gharbzadegi* and that they agreed with 80 percent of the book. [Translator's note]

12 Ghulamali Siyar (1923–1992) was a diplomat, translator, and writer. [Translator's note]

13 A Tehran neighborhood. [Translator's note]

14 A member of the Al-e Ahmad family. [Translator's note]

15 Aramesh Dustdar, a philosopher and friend of Al-e Ahmad's, who now lives in Germany. [Translator's note]

16 Ehsan Naraghi (1926–2012) was a prominent sociologist. The Institute for Social Studies and Research, which he founded at Tehran University in 1958, had a publishing arm. *Fashandak* is a sociological study of Taleqan, a province in north-central Iran, written by Houshang Pourkarim in 1962 and published by Naraghi with an introduction by Al-e Ahmad. [Translator's note]

17 Islam Kazemieh (1930–1997) was a short-story writer who fled to France after the Revolution and committed suicide in Paris. [Translator's note]

18 Bahman Mohasses (1931–2010) was a celebrated painter and sculptor, as well as a literary translator. He died in seclusion in Italy. [Translator's note]

19   A writer, translator, and journalist. [Translator's note]

20   Manouchehr Hezarkhani, a writer and translator. [Translator's note]

21   The name of the famous and widely read mystical poem by Sufi poet Jalal al-Din Rumi. [Translator's note]

22   The Biblical Museum. [Translator's note]

23   A magazine. [Translator's note]

24   The wife of Ghulamali Siyar. [Translator's note]

25   Masud Farzad (1906–1981) was a writer and translator who collaborated closely with preeminent writer Sadegh Hedayat in the 1930s, moved to London in 1942 to work for the BBC, and served as cultural attaché at the Iranian Embassy during Al-e Ahmad's visit. In a letter from January 4, Al-e Ahmad writes that it was Hedayat who animated Farzad's writing, and that after the former had died (by suicide in 1951) nothing remained. [Translator's note]

26   The pen name of poet Majdaldin Mirfakhrayi (1910–1972), who spent most of his life as a doctor in London. In a letter from January 4, Al-e Ahmad complains that Gilani spoke annoyingly incorrect Persian and, in general, has an outdated conception of Iranian society. [Translator's note]

27   *Barabbas* was a 1961 religious-epic film expanding on the career of Barabbas, from the Christian Passion narrative in the Gospel of Mark and other gospels. Al-e Ahmad writes in a letter from January 4 that he enjoyed the film. [Translator's note]

28   One of Al-e Ahmad's novels. [Translator's note]

29   Khalil Maleki (1903–1969), liberal socialist politician and mentor to Al-e Ahmad. [Translator's note]

30   Maria Martha Saran (1897–1976), known as Mary Saran, was a prominent socialist journalist and author. In 1933, she emigrated from her native Germany to England. [Translator's note]

31   In a letter from January 8, Daneshvar describes her visit to Maleki and his wife—"my only refuge"—and the emotional support they gave her. [Translator's note]

32   Farouhar (1928–1998) was a founder and leader of the Hezb-e Mellat-e Iran, a pan-Iranist opposition party. [Translator's note]

33   Fatemi (d. 2014) was a politician and intellectual close to ousted Prime Minister Mohammad Mosadegh. [Translator's note]

34   The brother of Khalil Maleki. [Translator's note]

35   The son of Khalil Maleki. [Translator's note]

36   Meir Ezri (1924–2015) was the Israeli ambassador to Iran from 1958 until 1973. [Translator's note]

37   Daneshvar's sister Victoria. [Translator's note]

38   Leila Riahi, Daneshvar's niece. [Translator's note]

39   Anushirvan Daneshvar, Simin Daneshvar's nephew. [Translator's note]

40   Tale (b. 1312) was a member of the Pan-Iranist party and a member of parliament. [Translator's note]

41   Colonel Ali-Naqi Vaziri (1887–1979), a musicologist and well-known tar player. [Translator's note]

42   This refers to an Azeri folktale about a girl who works for a month to wake a sleeping prince before her black slave takes her place at the last minute. The prince, upon waking, sees the slave and, thinking she had sat by his bedside the entire time, marries her, and the girl becomes the couple's servant. One day the prince goes to the market and buys a "patience stone doll." The girl tells her sad story to the doll, and the prince hears it, sends away the slave, and marries the girl. [Translator's note]

43   Victoria Daneshvar's husband and Simin's brother-in-law. [Translator's note]

44   An allusion to a proverb about starting work without planning first. [Translator's note]

45   Dariush Ashouri (b. 1938), a prominent Iranian intellectual who visited Israel the year before Al-e Ahmad and published an account of his visit in the magazine *Ketab-e Mah*. [Translator's note]

46   Simin Daneshvar's nephew. [Translator's note]

47   Ann Lambton (1912–2008) was a British historian and scholar of Persian at the School of Oriental and African Studies. She was a major proponent of the joint CIA-MI6 mission to topple Mohammad Mossadegh in 1953. [Translator's note]

48   Reza Shah (1878–1944) was the father of Mohammad Reza Shah and founder of the Pahlavi dynasty. He was buried in a tomb located near the shrine of Abdol Azim, a Shia saint and descendant of the second imam, Hassan. The tomb was destroyed following the 1979 revolution and is now a religious school. [Translator's note]

49   Hassan Arsanjani (1922–1969) was a journalist and politician who served as minister of agriculture from May 1961 until March 1963. He first proposed the land reforms

that the shah later co-opted as part of his White Revolution, which was put to a referendum on January 23, 1963. [Translator's note]

50 Daneshvar's older sister committed suicide. [Translator's note]

51 A London publisher. [Translator's note]

52 Ali Akbar Siassi (1896–1990) was head of Tehran University from 1942–1954. [Translator's note]

53 An official at the University of Tehran. [Translator's note]

54 The head of Al-e Ahmad's travel program. [Translator's note]

55 Bagher Kameli, a friend of Al-e Ahmad's. In a November 15 letter, Daneshvar describes his many efforts to help her fix her car. [Translator's note]

56 The pen name of Gholam Hossein Saedi (1936–1985). [Translator's note]

57 A relative of Al-e Ahmad's. [Translator's note]

58 Ezat Allah Negahban (1926–2009) was an eminent American-trained Iranian archaeologist. [Translator's note]

59 This phrase is a quote from the Persian poet Hafez (1325–1389) who referred to his beloved as "rock candy." [Translator's note]

60 Another University of Tehran official. [Translator's note]

61 Daneshvar's nephew. [Translator's note]

62 Badiozzaman Forouzanfar (1904–1970), a notable scholar of Persian literature at the University of Tehran. [Translator's note]

63 In her January 13 letter, Daneshvar discusses infidelity at length, hinting at Al-e Ahmad's own. [Translator's note]

64 Khadija, a successful businesswoman, was the Prophet Muhammad's first wife. [Translator's note]

65 The Prophet Muhammad's youngest and, tradition holds, his most beloved wife. [Translator's note]

66 Eprim Eshaq (1918–1998). [Translator's note]

67 Aly Salman Agha Khan (1911–1960), a famous playboy and horse enthusiast, was the son of Sultan Mahommed Shah, the third Agha Khan and leader of the Ismaili branch of Shia Islam. [Translator's note]

68   Al-e Ahmad's niece. [Translator's note]

69   Ebrahim Golestan (b. 1922) was a prominent Iranian left-wing writer and associate of Al-e Ahmad's. He divorced his wife Fakhri to pursue a relationship with the poet Forough Farrokhzad. [Translator's note]

70   Mirza Ali-Asghar Khan Hekmat Shirazi (1892–1980) was an Iranian diplomat and literary figure under Mohammad Reza Shah. [Translator's note]

71   Avery (1923–2008) was a scholar of Persian at Oxford whom Al-e Ahmad met during his stay in England. [Translator's note]

72   Mohammad-Ali Jamalzadeh (1892–1997) was one of the most prominent and influential Persian writers of the twentieth century. He spent most of his life in Berlin and Geneva. [Translator's note]

73   Miriam Merritt (d. 2004) studied creative writing at Stanford University with Daneshvar in 1952. Her novel *By Lions, Gladly Eaten* was published in 1955. [Translator's note]

74   Hannah Green (1927–1996) was a writer for *The New Yorker* and published two novels. [Translator's note]

75   Sadegh Hedayat (1903–1951) is the undisputed giant of modern Persian prose. The reference is to his satirical novel *Haji Agha*. [Translator's note]

76   In Persian, *fatir* is the word used for both unleavened bread and the Jewish holiday of Passover. [Translator's note]

77   According to the Qur'an's version of the story, the Egyptian woman who tries to seduce the pure and chaste Joseph is named Zuleikha. [Translator's note]

78   Perhaps a mistake, as Daneshvar's last letter is dated January 26. [Translator's note]

ACKNOWLEDGMENTS

It is a pleasure to thank all those who helped make this book a reality. For the use of their collections, my thanks to the helpful archivists and librarians at the Israel State Archives, the Israel National Library, the Asien-Afrika-Institut at the University of Hamburg, and the University of California, Berkeley. I am grateful to Zvi Rafiah and David Turgeman for sharing their time and their memories of the Israeli embassy in Tehran. For their corrections and comments on the translation, I owe a debt of gratitude to Ludwig Paul, Julia Rubanovich, Ramin Shaghaghi, Maryam Ozlati, and, most of all, to Mohammad Ghanoonparvar, who went over the first, rough draft with patience and a fine-tooth comb. The introduction owes what grace it has thanks to the suggestions of Nita Shechet, Daniel Noah Moses, Sheila Moussaiey, and Ali Ansari, whose encouragement came at just the right moment. Other friends and teachers, at home and abroad, too many to name, lent willing ears and sharp eyes.

No one could ask for a better agent than Diana Finch, nor a better editor than Joshua Ellison, whose idea all this was in the first place. An early version of Chapter One appeared in *Zeek*, and my thanks go to my editor there, Jo Ellen Green Kaiser. The Dorot Foundation provided crucial financial assistance, without which this book would never have become a reality.

To Tehila, for love and the accordion.

—SAMUEL THROPE

ABOUT THE AUTHORS

JALAL AL-E AHMAD was born to a clerical religious family in Tehran in 1923. A teacher all his life, he joined the Communist Tudeh Party in 1943 and quickly rose through its ranks, becoming a member of the party committee for Tehran, before breaking with the Tudeh in 1947 in protest over Soviet influence. Al-e Ahmad was an influential and prolific writer and social critic, whose body of work includes short stories, notably the collection *An Exchange of Visits*; novels including *By the Pen*, *The School Principal*, and *A Stone on a Grave*; travelogues including *A Straw in Mecca*, *A Journey to Russia*, and *A Journey to America*; anthropological studies; essays; reviews; and translations. His best-known work is *Gharbzadegi (Occidentosis)*, which has also been translated to English as *Weststruckness* and *Westoxification*, a cultural critique of Westernization in Iran. Al-e Ahmad was married to the novelist and translator Simin Daneshvar; the couple had no children. He died in 1969.

SIMIN DANESHVAR (born April 28, 1921, Shiraz, Iran—died March 8, 2012, Tehran, Iran), was an Iranian author who wrote the enduringly popular *Savūshūn* (1969; published in English as *Savushun: A Novel About Modern Iran*, 1990, and as *A Persian Requiem*, 1991), the first modern Persian-language novel written by a woman. In 1948, while Daneshvar was studying Persian literature at the University of Tehran (Ph.D., 1949), she published a short-story collection, *Atesh-e khamūsh* (*The Quenched Fire*), the first such book by a woman to come out in Iran. She published a second collection, *Shahrī chūn behesht* (1961; *A City as Paradise*) before embarking on *Savūshūn*. Later novels include *Jazīreh-ye Sargardānī* (1992; *The Island of Perplexity*) and *Sārebān-e sargardān* (2002; *Wandering Caravan Master*). She was also known for her translations into Persian of such writers as Anton Chekhov and Nathaniel Hawthorne. Daneshvar was married (1950–69) to noted writer and intellectual Jalal Al-e Ahmad and taught art history at the University of Tehran from the late 1950s until her retirement in 1979.

ABOUT THE TRANSLATOR

SAMUEL THROPE is a writer and translator based in Jerusalem. Born and raised in Arlington, Massachusetts, he earned his PhD at the University of California, Berkeley in 2012. He is the selector for the Islam and Middle East Collection at the National Library of Israel.

ABOUT THE INTRODUCER

BERNARD AVISHAI lives in Jerusalem and New Hampshire. He is a visiting professor of government at Dartmouth and an adjunct professor of business at Hebrew University. His most recent book is *Promiscuous: "Portnoy's Complaint" and Our Doomed Pursuit of Happiness*. He is also the author of *The Tragedy of Zionism* and *The Hebrew Republic*.